MINDFULNESS & HEALTH WATCH

YOUR 2023 WEEKLY JOURNAL

I hope you
enjoy this edition
of my latest book.

Gloria

THIS JOURNAL BELONGS TO

_____

... and I am grateful for my ...

_____

_____

_____

YOUR 2023 weekly journal has a fitness-health watch element.
If you journal and, also, monitor your fitness steps and
overall health, you will enjoy this edition.

THIS JOURNAL IS DEDICATED TO MY PARENTS,
Willie and Elaine Ham

I am grateful for my dad's love,

persevering nature, and amazing survivals.

When asked about his secret to a long and healthy life,
my dad shares this advice:

Love Everyone and Everything

Stay Busy!

Don't Go be Bed Angry

Today he resides in an assisted living facility (age 94)

I am grateful for my mother's love, giving nature, and caring ways.

In memory of my mother

1929 to 2021

Gloria (Ham) Petersen

"2023"

JANUARY

M	T	W	T	F	S	S
						1
2	3	4	5	6	7	8
9	10	11	12	13	14	15
16	17	18	19	20	21	22
23	24	25	26	27	28	29
30	31					

FEBRUARY

M	T	W	T	F	S	S
		1	2	3	4	5
6	7	8	9	10	11	12
13	14	15	16	17	18	19
20	21	22	23	24	25	26
27	28					

MARCH

M	T	W	T	F	S	S
		1	2	3	4	5
6	7	8	9	10	11	12
13	14	15	16	17	18	19
20	21	22	23	24	25	26
27	28	29	30	31		

APRIL

M	T	W	T	F	S	S
					1	2
3	4	5	6	7	8	9
10	11	12	13	14	15	16
17	18	19	20	21	22	23
24	25	26	27	28	29	30

MAY

M	T	W	T	F	S	S
1	2	3	4	5	6	7
8	9	10	11	12	13	14
15	16	17	18	19	20	21
22	23	24	25	26	27	28
29	30	31				

JUNE

M	T	W	T	F	S	S
			1	2	3	4
5	6	7	8	9	10	11
12	13	14	15	16	17	18
19	20	21	22	23	24	25
26	27	28	29	30		

JULY

M	T	W	T	F	S	S
					1	2
3	4	5	6	7	8	9
10	11	12	13	14	15	16
17	18	19	20	21	22	23
24	25	26	27	28	29	30
31						

AUGUST

M	T	W	T	F	S	S
	1	2	3	4	5	6
7	8	9	10	11	12	13
14	15	16	17	18	19	20
21	22	23	24	25	26	27
28	29	30	31			

SEPTEMBER

M	T	W	T	F	S	S
				1	2	3
4	5	6	7	8	9	10
11	12	13	14	15	16	17
18	19	20	21	22	23	24
25	26	27	28	29	30	

OCTOBER

M	T	W	T	F	S	S
						1
2	3	4	5	6	7	8
9	10	11	12	13	14	15
16	17	18	19	20	21	22
23	24	25	26	27	28	29
30	31					

NOVEMBER

M	T	W	T	F	S	S
		1	2	3	4	5
6	7	8	9	10	11	12
13	14	15	16	17	18	19
20	21	22	23	24	25	26
27	28	29	30			

DECEMBER

M	T	W	T	F	S	S
				1	2	3
4	5	6	7	8	9	10
11	12	13	14	15	16	17
18	19	20	21	22	23	24
25	26	27	28	29	30	31

DID YOU KNOW?

"Monday is the official international standard,"
This calendar begins on MONDAYS

WHY I CREATED THIS JOURNAL

When I was a teenager, I had a small, keyed diary where I wrote my joys and my innermost secrets. I loved my diary until the day my sister found it, accessed it, and read it. I was devastated and embarrassed. I never wrote in a diary again!

Fast forward to a time when, as an adult, I was dealing with an emotionally damaging relationship situation and was recuperating from a stabbing incident. At that point, I heard of Rick Warren's book "Purpose Filled Life", which also had a journal workbook. I read the book and then filled out every page in the journal. It helped me to transfer all the anger, hurt, and confusion from within my head and heart to paper. Although it didn't solve all of the problems I was dealing with, it helped me to destress by alleviating some of the lingering anger. Later, I utilized journaling to help me through a difficult family situation. One day I came across the journals and started to re-read them. Although some people might say re-reading is a lesson within itself, I found it devastating. It caused me to stirrup and relive memories I wanted to leave buried. So, I burned them! Yes, I felt better afterward.

Years later, and on a more positive note, I attended a Global Women's Peace Network luncheon. We were all given a "Gratitude Diary" written by Melanie Spears as a gift. It was beautifully done, felt special, and re-ignited my desire to journal again. I enjoyed Melanie's sharing of herself in personal notes throughout the diary, her approach to recording daily thoughts, and the spiritual guidance it also offered were uplifting. Please visit my recap of her journal on my website:

- GloriaPetersen.com

- Click on ... Blogs and Articles | Inspire to Aspire | Why Gratitude

Melanie's "Gratitude Diary" inspired me to continue journeying in a more positive way. I continue to journal to help myself get beyond life's obstacles and disappointments as they occur and to stay focused on the positive aspects of my life.

My son gifted me a smartwatch for Christmas. It inspired me to start challenging myself with a daily recording of my steps. I should also mention that a recent physical indicated that I had an oxygen flow to the brain concern, and daily walking was highly recommended. Although these watches have apps that record your daily activities, I started recording my step activity in the margin of my journal so I could have it at-a-glance. As we have evolved into a Fitbit-type society, I thought, why not add a "Health Watch" box to each day? This way we are giving ourselves both a mental and physical weekly checkup. They are both important to one's well-being. Agree? And yes, this new habit of walking and monitoring my steps did improve the oxygen flow to my brain. Sold on daily walks!

Before I decided to publish my own version of a journal, I went to Barnes & Noble's journal and diary sections and literally sat on the floor as I scanned through all the pages. I just couldn't find a journal that had the elements I was seeking because I now had my own ideas on how I wanted MY journal to work. Hence, this journal was developed. Why not share with all of you?

Let's Get Started

There are numerous ways for YOU to ACCESS ways to inject or cultivate an attitude of positivity into your daily routine. They range from books, videos, tapes, retreats, and social media, to participating in retreats and seminars. What's important is to have a routine that allows you reflective time every day. By utilizing a diary or incorporating journaling, viewing a video, and/or listening to an audio, you are creating a helpful and healthy pattern.

> *Note:* There is a slight difference between a diary (records daily data) and a journal (reflection and aspiration). Both are used to keep personal records or daily thoughts. Both can be fancy covers with lined pages, or they can be written in a workbook style that helps engage or direct you.

Sharing MY Routine

Upon waking every morning, I begin with a routine that helps me set a positive tone. Sometimes I disperse this routine throughout the day because life has its unexpected diversions. This habit has been especially helpful when I'm dealing with adversity. **You create yours!**

Upon wakening … "I" …

- Brush my teeth to refresh my mouth and stimulate my taste buds.

- Make coffee and eat two dates (which makes my coffee taste better)

- Turn on YouTube and watch five or ten minutes of gratitude while enjoying my coffee. For example: "Today I am grateful for _____"

- Say my prayer for the day and reflect by asking myself a few questions; then listen to my inner voice for an answer. My prayers always include a prayer for those dealing with physical and/or emotional challenges as **I recite: "…keep the faith, have hope and look for better days to come."**

- Read a short spiritual excerpt or chapter from a positive mindset book source.

- Record in my journal.

- Engage in ten minutes of Yoga stretch followed by a one-minute plank to strengthen my lower back, and three minutes of inversion (upside down exercise position) to get my body moving, blood flow engaged, and oxygen flowing. (Make sure that this position is approved by your doctor.)

- Have Breakfast…ALWAYS. This wakes my metabolism.

- Walk for 30 to 60 minutes.

- Turn on my laptop and check my calendar for the day. I'm ready!

- Record my steps at the end of the day.

- When I retire for the day, I set my timer and select a YouTube mental refresh video, lasting for at least an hour. I'm in a deep sleep within minutes every night. **Best sleeping pill alternative ever!**

Yes, this does mean that I get up extra early. You decide what part of the day works best for you and set your routine. You may have to break your routine into two or three sessions throughout the day.

As a bonus, visit my website GloriaPetersen.com, click on Author, then Mindfulness Journal. I invite you to share how journaling has helped you. We will be creating a community of inspirational sharing.

YOUR SEVEN DAYS OF MINDFULNESS

Everyone's basic need is to be respected, validated, and appreciated. Start with YOU!

Intention

Focus on Desired Accomplishments

An intention **is an aim or purpose, something you plan to do or achieve** — then do it. It's that sense of accomplishment that is so validating. And, if you don't finish, just add that intention to the next day until finished. Things happen and interfere with our best intentions. It can be a personal or business/career-related mission. Finish the intention or create a new one. It's important to keep moving ahead.

Gratitude

Appreciate Everything and Everybody

Gratitude **is one of many positive emotions**. It's about focusing on what's good in our lives and being thankful for the things we have. Gratitude is pausing to notice and appreciate the things that we often take for granted, like having a place to live, food, clean water, friends, family, and even computer access. Begin your day with gratitude and end your day acknowledging something you experienced in a grateful way.

Affirmation

Reinforce Self Truth

An affirmation **is to affirm or assert that something exists or is true**. It is also about your truth about yourself. Go deep within yourself and discover your truths before judging another. What do you believe to be true and then ask yourself why, does it make sense, and does it need to be adjusted? In other words, "who am I"? Go deep!

Visualization

Create Your Actuality

Visualization **is creating a mental picture of how you want something to be or to evolve.** Visualization is taking an idea to fruition; it's the key to inventions and change. How do you want to see your life evolve? Be flexible! Sometimes the visual picture needs to change or be reworked. Keep creating and recreating.

Kindness

Extend and Receive Good Deeds

Kindness **is how you treat yourself and others**. Treating people with kindness and respect makes the world a better place and sets a better example. No matter how unfair or insensitive someone has been to you, you treat them with kindness. It can be hard, but it is necessary. The greatest need is kindness. Just be caring and decent to others. Use every opportunity to extend a random act of kindness. Kindness is win-win and always sets a better example! Become a role model to others with your kindness.

Wisdom

Share Age-Long Experiences

Wisdom **is the ability or result of an ability to think and act utilizing knowledge, experience, understanding, common sense, and insight**. It allows us to experience knowledge, take risks, and engage one's intuition for a full experience. Wisdom is not just about age, although in some cultures age gives the right to wisdom. It's about making good, solid decisions based on experience and foresight. Then, share your wisdom with others.

Spirituality

Spirituality **is the quality of being concerned with the human spirit or soul as opposed to material or physical things.** It's about the breath and quiet moments that allow us to go deep within ourselves to find answers and alleviate stress. It is the shift in priorities that allows us to embrace our spirituality in a more profound way. It's how something as simple as the "breath" can create calmness.

A Note About the *Quotes* Throughout This Journal

Every effort was made to select quotes that are original and that fit the theme for that month. Some quotes DO NOT have an outside source because they are thoughts that I want to share that I jotted down and kept.

HEALTH WATCH

A healthy happy lifestyle is made up of both mental and physical well-being. Journals are typically all about thinking positively. We all know the importance of incorporating exercise into our daily routine. Why not record both?

HEALTH Watch
Steps Achieved: ....
Distance Walked: ....
Calories Burned: ....
Mindfulness Minutes: ....

At the end of the day, record your smartwatch or Fitbit progress based on steps achieved, calories burned, and time spent on mindfulness. This is a great way to stay motivated by recording your progress. Before you know it, you are doing more than you imagined.

What I learned this week about myself, others, and/or the world around me:

This page is your opportunity to appreciate YOU! Consider the following:

☐ The highlight of my week was ....

☐ The three things that made the biggest difference for me this week ...

☐ How I helped someone get through a difficult moment or situation ...

☐ How I helped myself stay calm (destress) during a difficult or challenging moment ...

☐ What I learned ...What I saw ... What I experienced ... New ideas that emerged ...

Exercises that I performed this week:

If you prefer not to record steps, then jot down your exercise routine. Just keep moving.

This week's healthy eating food choices:

Jot down your healthy diet habits at the end of the week. What new healthy foods did you try? Did you increase your vegetable intake and minimize non-foods (processed foods)? If you have a sweet tooth, write down that today you said NO to a candy bar. Whatever keeps you eating healthy.

JANUARY 2023

Sunday, January 1

*With every new year, it is time to **reboot**:*
***REFLECT** on what worked, **REFOCUS** utilizing new ideas, then **RENEW** your approach.*
Allow each NEW Season to be your guide.

MONDAY, JANUARY 2

Intention: *Focus on Desired Accomplishment*

HEALTH Watch
Steps Achieved:
Distance Walked:
Calories Burned:
Mindfulness Minutes:

TUESDAY, JANUARY 3

Gratitude: *Appreciate Everything and Everybody*

HEALTH Watch
Steps Achieved:
Distance Walked:
Calories Burned:
Mindfulness Minutes:

WEDNESDAY, JANUARY 4

Affirmation: *Reinforce Self Truth*

HEALTH Watch
Steps Achieved:
Distance Walked:
Calories Burned:
Mindfulness Minutes:

THURSDAY, JANUARY 5

Visualization: *Create Your Actuality*

HEALTH Watch
Steps Achieved: ....
Distance Walked: ....
Calories Burned: ....
Mindfulness Minutes: ....

FRIDAY, JANUARY 6

Kindness: *Extend and Receive Good Deeds*

HEALTH Watch
Steps Achieved: ....
Distance Walked: ....
Calories Burned: ....
Mindfulness Minutes: ....

SATURDAY, JANUARY 7

Wisdom: *Share Age-Long Experiences*

HEALTH Watch
Steps Achieved: ....
Distance Walked: ....
Calories Burned: ....
Mindfulness Minutes: ....

SUNDAY, JANUARY 8

Spirituality: *Have a Heart Centered Mindset*

HEALTH Watch
Steps Achieved: ....
Distance Walked: ....
Calories Burned: ....
Mindfulness Minutes: ....

What I learned this week about myself, others, and/or
the world around me:

_____

_____

_____

_____

_____

_____

_____

Exercises that I performed this week:

_____

_____

_____

_____

This week's healthy eating food choices:

_____

_____

_____

_____

JANUARY 2023

Never underestimate the power you have to take your life in a new direction.
—Germany Kent

MONDAY, JANUARY 9

Intention: *Focus on Desired Accomplishment*

HEALTH Watch
Steps Achieved:
Distance Walked:
Calories Burned:
Mindfulness Minutes:

TUESDAY, JANUARY 10

Gratitude: *Appreciate Everything and Everybody*

HEALTH Watch
Steps Achieved:
Distance Walked:
Calories Burned:
Mindfulness Minutes:

WEDNESDAY, JANUARY 11

Affirmation: *Reinforce Self Truth*

HEALTH Watch
Steps Achieved:
Distance Walked:
Calories Burned:
Mindfulness Minutes:

THURSDAY, JANUARY 12

Visualization: *Create Your Actuality*

HEALTH Watch
Steps Achieved: ....
Distance Walked: ....
Calories Burned: ....
Mindfulness Minutes: ....

FRIDAY, JANUARY 13

Kindness: *Extend and Receive Good Deeds*

HEALTH Watch
Steps Achieved: ....
Distance Walked: ....
Calories Burned: ....
Mindfulness Minutes: ....

SATURDAY, JANUARY 14

Wisdom: *Share Age-Long Experiences*

HEALTH Watch
Steps Achieved: ....
Distance Walked: ....
Calories Burned: ....
Mindfulness Minutes: ....

SUNDAY, JANUARY 15

Spirituality: *Have a Heart Centered Mindset*

HEALTH Watch
Steps Achieved: ....
Distance Walked: ....
Calories Burned: ....
Mindfulness Minutes: ....

What I learned this week about myself, others, and/or
the world around me:

_____
_____
_____
_____
_____
_____
_____

Exercises that I performed this week:

_____
_____
_____
_____

This week's healthy eating food choices:

_____
_____
_____
_____

JANUARY 2023

If I cannot do great things, I can do small things in a great way.
—Martin Luther King Jr.

MONDAY, JANUARY 16

Intention: *Focus on Desired Accomplishment*

HEALTH Watch
Steps Achieved:
Distance Walked:
Calories Burned:
Mindfulness Minutes:

TUESDAY, JANUARY 17

Gratitude: *Appreciate Everything and Everybody*

HEALTH Watch
Steps Achieved:
Distance Walked:
Calories Burned:
Mindfulness Minutes:

WEDNESDAY, JANUARY 18

Affirmation: *Reinforce Self Truth*

HEALTH Watch
Steps Achieved:
Distance Walked:
Calories Burned:
Mindfulness Minutes:

THURSDAY, JANUARY 19

Visualization: *Create Your Actuality*

HEALTH Watch
Steps Achieved:
Distance Walked:
Calories Burned:
Mindfulness Minutes:

FRIDAY, JANUARY 20

Kindness: *Extend and Receive Good Deeds*

HEALTH Watch
Steps Achieved:
Distance Walked:
Calories Burned:
Mindfulness Minutes:

SATURDAY, JANUARY 21

Wisdom: *Share Age-Long Experiences*

HEALTH Watch
Steps Achieved:
Distance Walked:
Calories Burned:
Mindfulness Minutes:

SUNDAY, JANUARY 22

Spirituality: *Have a Heart Centered Mindset*

HEALTH Watch
Steps Achieved:
Distance Walked:
Calories Burned:
Mindfulness Minutes:

What I learned this week about myself, others, and/or the world around me:

_____

_____

_____

_____

_____

_____

_____

Exercises that I performed this week:

_____

_____

_____

_____

This week's healthy eating food choices:

_____

_____

_____

_____

JANUARY 2023

Prosperity is being debt free.
Wellness is a healthy mind and body. Love is the ability to love.

MONDAY, JANUARY 23

Intention: *Focus on Desired Accomplishment*

HEALTH Watch
Steps Achieved:
Distance Walked:
Calories Burned:
Mindfulness Minutes:

TUESDAY, JANUARY 24

Gratitude: *Appreciate Everything and Everybody*

HEALTH Watch
Steps Achieved:
Distance Walked:
Calories Burned:
Mindfulness Minutes:

WEDNESDAY, JANUARY 25

Affirmation: *Reinforce Self Truth*

HEALTH Watch
Steps Achieved:
Distance Walked:
Calories Burned:
Mindfulness Minutes:

THURSDAY, JANUARY 26

Visualization: *Create Your Actuality*

HEALTH Watch	
Steps Achieved:	
Distance Walked:	
Calories Burned:	
Mindfulness Minutes:	

FRIDAY, JANUARY 27

Kindness: *Extend and Receive Good Deeds*

HEALTH Watch	
Steps Achieved:	
Distance Walked:	
Calories Burned:	
Mindfulness Minutes:	

SATURDAY, JANUARY 28

Wisdom: *Share Age-Long Experiences*

HEALTH Watch	
Steps Achieved:	
Distance Walked:	
Calories Burned:	
Mindfulness Minutes:	

SUNDAY, JANUARY 29

Spirituality: *Have a Heart Centered Mindset*

HEALTH Watch	
Steps Achieved:	
Distance Walked:	
Calories Burned:	
Mindfulness Minutes:	

What I learned this week about myself, others, and/or the world around me:

_____

_____

_____

_____

_____

_____

_____

Exercises that I performed this week:

_____

_____

_____

_____

This week's healthy eating food choices:

_____

_____

_____

_____

JANUARY – FEBRUARY 2023

We do not remember days, we remember moments.
The richness of life lies in memories we have forgotten.
—Cesare Pavese

MONDAY, JANUARY 30

Intention: *Focus on Desired Accomplishment*

	HEALTH Watch
	Steps Achieved:
	Distance Walked:
	Calories Burned:
	Mindfulness Minutes:

TUESDAY, *JANUARY 31*

Gratitude: *Appreciate Everything and Everybody*

	HEALTH Watch
	Steps Achieved:
	Distance Walked:
	Calories Burned:
	Mindfulness Minutes:

WEDNESDAY, FEBRUARY 1

Affirmation: *Reinforce Self Truth*

	HEALTH Watch
	Steps Achieved:
	Distance Walked:
	Calories Burned:
	Mindfulness Minutes:

THURSDAY, FEBRUARY 2

Visualization: *Create Your Actuality*

HEALTH Watch
Steps Achieved:
Distance Walked:
Calories Burned:
Mindfulness Minutes:

FRIDAY, FEBRUARY 3

Kindness: *Extend and Receive Good Deeds*

HEALTH Watch
Steps Achieved:
Distance Walked:
Calories Burned:
Mindfulness Minutes:

SATURDAY, FEBRUARY 4

Wisdom: *Share Age-Long Experiences*

HEALTH Watch
Steps Achieved:
Distance Walked:
Calories Burned:
Mindfulness Minutes:

SUNDAY, FEBRUARY 5

Spirituality: *Have a Heart Centered Mindset*

HEALTH Watch
Steps Achieved:
Distance Walked:
Calories Burned:
Mindfulness Minutes:

What I learned this week about myself, others, and/or
the world around me:

_____

_____

_____

_____

_____

_____

_____

_____

Exercises that I performed this week:

_____

_____

_____

_____

This week's healthy eating food choices:

_____

_____

_____

_____

FEBRUARY 2023

Don't worry when you are not recognized but strive to be worthy of recognition.
—Abraham Lincoln

MONDAY, FEBRUARY 6

Intention: *Focus on Desired Accomplishment*

HEALTH Watch
Steps Achieved:
Distance Walked:
Calories Burned:
Mindfulness Minutes:

TUESDAY, FEBRUARY 7

Gratitude: *Appreciate Everything and Everybody*

HEALTH Watch
Steps Achieved:
Distance Walked:
Calories Burned:
Mindfulness Minutes:

WEDNESDAY, FEBRUARY 8

Affirmation: *Reinforce Self Truth*

HEALTH Watch
Steps Achieved:
Distance Walked:
Calories Burned:
Mindfulness Minutes:

THURSDAY, FEBRUARY 9

Visualization: *Create Your Actuality*

HEALTH Watch
Steps Achieved: ....
Distance Walked: ....
Calories Burned: ....
Mindfulness Minutes: ....

FRIDAY, FEBRUARY 10

Kindness: *Extend and Receive Good Deeds*

HEALTH Watch
Steps Achieved: ....
Distance Walked: ....
Calories Burned: ....
Mindfulness Minutes: ....

SATURDAY, FEBRUARY 11

Wisdom: *Share Age-Long Experiences*

HEALTH Watch
Steps Achieved: ....
Distance Walked: ....
Calories Burned: ....
Mindfulness Minutes: ....

SUNDAY, FEBRUARY 12

Spirituality: *Have a Heart Centered Mindset*

HEALTH Watch
Steps Achieved: ....
Distance Walked: ....
Calories Burned: ....
Mindfulness Minutes: ....

What I learned this week about myself, others, and/or the world around me:

....

....

....

....

....

....

....

Exercises that I performed this week:

....

....

....

....

This week's healthy eating food choices:

....

....

....

....

FEBRUARY 2023

Valentine's Day is a reminder for us to stop and pay attention to those we care about.
—Lisa Merlo-Booth

MONDAY, FEBRUARY 13

Intention: *Focus on Desired Accomplishment*

HEALTH Watch
Steps Achieved:
Distance Walked:
Calories Burned:
Mindfulness Minutes:

TUESDAY, FEBRUARY 14

Gratitude: *Appreciate Everything and Everybody*

HEALTH Watch
Steps Achieved:
Distance Walked:
Calories Burned:
Mindfulness Minutes:

WEDNESDAY, FEBRUARY 15

Affirmation: *Reinforce Self Truth*

HEALTH Watch
Steps Achieved:
Distance Walked:
Calories Burned:
Mindfulness Minutes:

THURSDAY, FEBRUARY 16

Visualization: *Create Your Actuality*

<table>
<tr><td></td><td colspan="2">HEALTH Watch</td></tr>
<tr><td></td><td>Steps Achieved:</td><td></td></tr>
<tr><td></td><td>Distance Walked:</td><td></td></tr>
<tr><td></td><td>Calories Burned:</td><td></td></tr>
<tr><td></td><td>Mindfulness Minutes:</td><td></td></tr>
</table>

FRIDAY, FEBRUARY 17

Kindness: *Extend and Receive Good Deeds*

<table>
<tr><td></td><td colspan="2">HEALTH Watch</td></tr>
<tr><td></td><td>Steps Achieved:</td><td></td></tr>
<tr><td></td><td>Distance Walked:</td><td></td></tr>
<tr><td></td><td>Calories Burned:</td><td></td></tr>
<tr><td></td><td>Mindfulness Minutes:</td><td></td></tr>
</table>

SATURDAY, FEBRUARY 18

Wisdom: *Share Age-Long Experiences*

<table>
<tr><td></td><td colspan="2">HEALTH Watch</td></tr>
<tr><td></td><td>Steps Achieved:</td><td></td></tr>
<tr><td></td><td>Distance Walked:</td><td></td></tr>
<tr><td></td><td>Calories Burned:</td><td></td></tr>
<tr><td></td><td>Mindfulness Minutes:</td><td></td></tr>
</table>

SUNDAY, FEBRUARY 19

Spirituality: *Have a Heart Centered Mindset*

<table>
<tr><td></td><td colspan="2">HEALTH Watch</td></tr>
<tr><td></td><td>Steps Achieved:</td><td></td></tr>
<tr><td></td><td>Distance Walked:</td><td></td></tr>
<tr><td></td><td>Calories Burned:</td><td></td></tr>
<tr><td></td><td>Mindfulness Minutes:</td><td></td></tr>
</table>

What I learned this week about myself, others, and/or the world around me:

_____

_____

_____

_____

_____

_____

_____

_____

Exercises that I performed this week:

_____

_____

_____

_____

_____

This week's healthy eating food choices:

_____

_____

_____

_____

_____

FEBRUARY 2023

You can't wait until life isn't hard to be happy
—Jane "Nightbird" *AGT 6/7/21 Golden Buzzer Winner*
(A cancer victim who shared her gift of song and stayed positive to her last breath)

MONDAY, FEBRUARY 20

Intention: *Focus on Desired Accomplishment*

....
....
....
....
....
....

HEALTH Watch
Steps Achieved: ....
Distance Walked: ....
Calories Burned: ....
Mindfulness Minutes: ....

TUESDAY, FEBRUARY 21

Gratitude: *Appreciate Everything and Everybody*

....
....
....
....
....
....

HEALTH Watch
Steps Achieved: ....
Distance Walked: ....
Calories Burned: ....
Mindfulness Minutes: ....

WEDNESDAY, FEBRUARY 22

Affirmation: *Reinforce Self Truth*

....
....
....
....
....
....

HEALTH Watch
Steps Achieved: ....
Distance Walked: ....
Calories Burned: ....
Mindfulness Minutes: ....

THURSDAY, FEBRUARY 23

Visualization: *Create Your Actuality*

HEALTH Watch
Steps Achieved: ....
Distance Walked: ....
Calories Burned: ....
Mindfulness Minutes: ....

FRIDAY, FEBRUARY 24

Kindness: *Extend and Receive Good Deeds*

HEALTH Watch
Steps Achieved: ....
Distance Walked: ....
Calories Burned: ....
Mindfulness Minutes: ....

SATURDAY, FEBRUARY 25

Wisdom: *Share Age-Long Experiences*

HEALTH Watch
Steps Achieved: ....
Distance Walked: ....
Calories Burned: ....
Mindfulness Minutes: ....

SUNDAY, FEBRUARY 26

Spirituality: *Have a Heart Centered Mindset*

HEALTH Watch
Steps Achieved: ....
Distance Walked: ....
Calories Burned: ....
Mindfulness Minutes: ....

What I learned this week about myself, others, and/or
the world around me:

_____

_____

_____

_____

_____

_____

Exercises that I performed this week:

_____

_____

_____

_____

This week's healthy eating food choices:

_____

_____

_____

_____

FEBRUARY – MARCH 2023

Every adversity, every failure, every Heartbreak, carries with It
The seed of an equal or greater benefit
— Napoleon Hill

MONDAY, FEBRUARY 27

Intention: *Focus on Desired Accomplishment*

HEALTH Watch
Steps Achieved:
Distance Walked:
Calories Burned:
Mindfulness Minutes:

TUESDAY, FEBRUARY 28

Gratitude: *Appreciate Everything and Everybody*

HEALTH Watch
Steps Achieved:
Distance Walked:
Calories Burned:
Mindfulness Minutes:

WEDNESDAY, MARCH 1

Affirmation: *Reinforce Self Truth*

HEALTH Watch
Steps Achieved:
Distance Walked:
Calories Burned:
Mindfulness Minutes:

THURSDAY, MARCH 2

Visualization: *Create Your Actuality*

HEALTH Watch
Steps Achieved:
Distance Walked:
Calories Burned:
Mindfulness Minutes:

FRIDAY, MARCH 3

Kindness: *Extend and Receive Good Deeds*

HEALTH Watch
Steps Achieved:
Distance Walked:
Calories Burned:
Mindfulness Minutes:

SATURDAY, MARCH 4

Wisdom: *Share Age-Long Experiences*

HEALTH Watch
Steps Achieved:
Distance Walked:
Calories Burned:
Mindfulness Minutes:

SUNDAY, MARCH 5

Spirituality: *Have a Heart Centered Mindset*

HEALTH Watch
Steps Achieved:
Distance Walked:
Calories Burned:
Mindfulness Minutes:

What I learned this week about myself, others, and/or
the world around me:

_____

_____

_____

_____

_____

_____

_____

Exercises that I performed this week:

_____

_____

_____

_____

_____

This week's healthy eating food choices:

_____

_____

_____

_____

MARCH 2023

When we see the wisdom of change, we will find contentment.
—Todd Cornell

MONDAY, MARCH 6

Intention: *Focus on Desired Accomplishment*

....

HEALTH Watch	
Steps Achieved:	....
Distance Walked:	....
Calories Burned:	....
Mindfulness Minutes:	....

TUESDAY, MARCH 7

Gratitude: *Appreciate Everything and Everybody*

....

HEALTH Watch	
Steps Achieved:	....
Distance Walked:	....
Calories Burned:	....
Mindfulness Minutes:	....

WEDNESDAY, MARCH 8

Affirmation: *Reinforce Self Truth*

....

HEALTH Watch	
Steps Achieved:	....
Distance Walked:	....
Calories Burned:	....
Mindfulness Minutes:	....

THURSDAY, MARCH 9

Visualization: *Create Your Actuality*

HEALTH Watch
Steps Achieved:
Distance Walked:
Calories Burned:
Mindfulness Minutes:

FRIDAY, MARCH 10

Kindness: *Extend and Receive Good Deeds*

HEALTH Watch
Steps Achieved:
Distance Walked:
Calories Burned:
Mindfulness Minutes:

SATURDAY, MARCH 11

Wisdom: *Share Age-Long Experiences*

HEALTH Watch
Steps Achieved:
Distance Walked:
Calories Burned:
Mindfulness Minutes:

SUNDAY, MARCH 12

Spirituality: *Have a Heart Centered Mindset*

HEALTH Watch
Steps Achieved:
Distance Walked:
Calories Burned:
Mindfulness Minutes:

What I learned this week about myself, others, and/or
the world around me:

_____

_____

_____

_____

_____

_____

_____

Exercises that I performed this week:

_____

_____

_____

_____

This week's healthy eating food choices:

_____

_____

_____

_____

MARCH 2023

Meditation is focused thinking. Make it positive thinking.
—Unknown

MONDAY, MARCH 13

Intention: *Focus on Desired Accomplishment*

HEALTH Watch
Steps Achieved:
Distance Walked:
Calories Burned:
Mindfulness Minutes:

TUESDAY, MARCH 14

Gratitude: *Appreciate Everything and Everybody*

HEALTH Watch
Steps Achieved:
Distance Walked:
Calories Burned:
Mindfulness Minutes:

WEDNESDAY, MARCH 15

Affirmation: *Reinforce Self Truth*

HEALTH Watch
Steps Achieved:
Distance Walked:
Calories Burned:
Mindfulness Minutes:

THURSDAY, MARCH 16

Visualization: *Create Your Actuality*

....

HEALTH Watch
Steps Achieved: ....
Distance Walked: ....
Calories Burned: ....
Mindfulness Minutes: ....

FRIDAY, MARCH 17

Kindness: *Extend and Receive Good Deeds*

....

HEALTH Watch
Steps Achieved: ....
Distance Walked: ....
Calories Burned: ....
Mindfulness Minutes: ....

SATURDAY, MARCH 18

Wisdom: *Share Age-Long Experiences*

....

HEALTH Watch
Steps Achieved: ....
Distance Walked: ....
Calories Burned: ....
Mindfulness Minutes: ....

SUNDAY, MARCH 19

Spirituality: *Have a Heart Centered Mindset*

....

HEALTH Watch
Steps Achieved: ....
Distance Walked: ....
Calories Burned: ....
Mindfulness Minutes: ....

What I learned this week about myself, others, and/or
the world around me:

....
....
....
....
....
....
....
....

Exercises that I performed this week:

....
....
....
....
....

This week's healthy eating food choices:

....
....
....
....
....

MARCH 2023

Our prime purpose in this life is to help others.
And if you can't help them, at least don't hurt them.
—Dalai Lama

MONDAY, MARCH 20

Intention: *Focus on Desired Accomplishment*

....
....
....
....
....

HEALTH Watch
Steps Achieved: ....
Distance Walked: ....
Calories Burned: ....
Mindfulness Minutes: ....

TUESDAY, MARCH 21

Spring: A time of new growth and renewal
Gratitude: *Appreciate Everything and Everybody*

....
....
....
....
....

HEALTH Watch
Steps Achieved: ....
Distance Walked: ....
Calories Burned: ....
Mindfulness Minutes: ....

WEDNESDAY, MARCH 22

Affirmation: *Reinforce Self Truth*

....
....
....
....
....

HEALTH Watch
Steps Achieved: ....
Distance Walked: ....
Calories Burned: ....
Mindfulness Minutes: ....

THURSDAY, MARCH 23

Visualization: *Create Your Actuality*

HEALTH Watch
Steps Achieved:
Distance Walked:
Calories Burned:
Mindfulness Minutes:

FRIDAY, MARCH 24

Kindness: *Extend and Receive Good Deeds*

HEALTH Watch
Steps Achieved:
Distance Walked:
Calories Burned:
Mindfulness Minutes:

SATURDAY, MARCH 25

Wisdom: *Share Age-Long Experiences*

HEALTH Watch
Steps Achieved:
Distance Walked:
Calories Burned:
Mindfulness Minutes:

SUNDAY, MARCH 26

Spirituality: *Have a Heart Centered Mindset*

HEALTH Watch
Steps Achieved:
Distance Walked:
Calories Burned:
Mindfulness Minutes:

What I learned this week about myself, others, and/or
the world around me:

_____

_____

_____

_____

_____

_____

Exercises that I performed this week:

_____

_____

_____

_____

This week's healthy eating food choices:

_____

_____

_____

_____

MARCH – APRIL 2023

Knowledge is having the facts. Wisdom is applying those facts to life. Without our wisdom our knowledge is useless. We must learn how to live out what we know and experience.

MONDAY, MARCH 27

Intention: *Focus on Desired Accomplishment*

HEALTH Watch
Steps Achieved:
Distance Walked:
Calories Burned:
Mindfulness Minutes:

TUESDAY, MARCH 28

Gratitude: *Appreciate Everything and Everybody*

HEALTH Watch
Steps Achieved:
Distance Walked:
Calories Burned:
Mindfulness Minutes:

WEDNESDAY, MARCH 29

Affirmation: *Reinforce Self Truth*

HEALTH Watch
Steps Achieved:
Distance Walked:
Calories Burned:
Mindfulness Minutes:

THURSDAY, MARCH 30

Visualization: *Create Your Actuality*

....

....

....

....

....

....

HEALTH Watch	
Steps Achieved:	....
Distance Walked:	....
Calories Burned:	....
Mindfulness Minutes:	....

FRIDAY, MARCH 31

Kindness: *Extend and Receive Good Deeds*

....

....

....

....

....

....

HEALTH Watch	
Steps Achieved:	....
Distance Walked:	....
Calories Burned:	....
Mindfulness Minutes:	....

SATURDAY, APRIL 1

Wisdom: *Share Age-Long Experiences*

....

....

....

....

....

....

HEALTH Watch	
Steps Achieved:	....
Distance Walked:	....
Calories Burned:	....
Mindfulness Minutes:	....

SUNDAY, APRIL 2

Spirituality: *Have a Heart Centered Mindset*

....

....

....

....

....

....

HEALTH Watch	
Steps Achieved:	....
Distance Walked:	....
Calories Burned:	....
Mindfulness Minutes:	....

What I learned this week about myself, others, and/or the world around me:

_____

_____

_____

_____

_____

_____

_____

Exercises that I performed this week:

_____

_____

_____

_____

_____

This week's healthy eating food choices:

_____

_____

_____

_____

APRIL 2023

Easter is a time when GOD turned the inevitability of death into the invincibility of life.
—Craig D. Lounsbrough

MONDAY, APRIL 3

Intention: *Focus on Desired Accomplishment*

HEALTH Watch
Steps Achieved: ....
Distance Walked: ....
Calories Burned: ....
Mindfulness Minutes: ....

TUESDAY, APRIL 4

Gratitude: *Appreciate Everything and Everybody*

HEALTH Watch
Steps Achieved: ....
Distance Walked: ....
Calories Burned: ....
Mindfulness Minutes: ....

WEDNESDAY, APRIL 5

Affirmation: *Reinforce Self Truth*

HEALTH Watch
Steps Achieved: ....
Distance Walked: ....
Calories Burned: ....
Mindfulness Minutes: ....

THURSDAY, APRIL 6

Visualization: *Create Your Actuality*

....
....
....
....
....
....

HEALTH Watch
Steps Achieved: ....
Distance Walked: ....
Calories Burned: ....
Mindfulness Minutes: ....

FRIDAY, APRIL 7

Kindness: *Extend and Receive Good Deeds*

....
....
....
....
....
....

HEALTH Watch
Steps Achieved: ....
Distance Walked: ....
Calories Burned: ....
Mindfulness Minutes: ....

SATURDAY, APRIL 8

Wisdom: *Share Age-Long Experiences*

....
....
....
....
....
....

HEALTH Watch
Steps Achieved: ....
Distance Walked: ....
Calories Burned: ....
Mindfulness Minutes: ....

SUNDAY, APRIL 9

Spirituality: *Have a Heart Centered Mindset*

....
....
....
....
....
....

HEALTH Watch
Steps Achieved: ....
Distance Walked: ....
Calories Burned: ....
Mindfulness Minutes: ....

What I learned this week about myself, others, and/or
the world around me:

_____

_____

_____

_____

_____

_____

_____

Exercises that I performed this week:

_____

_____

_____

_____

This week's healthy eating food choices:

_____

_____

_____

_____

APRIL 2023

The Easter egg symbolizes our ability to break out of the hardened,
protective shell we've surrounded ourselves with.
—Siobhan Shaw

MONDAY, APRIL 10

Intention: *Focus on Desired Accomplishment*

HEALTH Watch
Steps Achieved:
Distance Walked:
Calories Burned:
Mindfulness Minutes:

TUESDAY, APRIL 11

Gratitude: *Appreciate Everything and Everybody*

HEALTH Watch
Steps Achieved:
Distance Walked:
Calories Burned:
Mindfulness Minutes:

WEDNESDAY, APRIL 12

Affirmation: *Reinforce Self Truth*

HEALTH Watch
Steps Achieved:
Distance Walked:
Calories Burned:
Mindfulness Minutes:

THURSDAY, APRIL 13

Visualization: *Create Your Actuality*

HEALTH Watch
Steps Achieved:
Distance Walked:
Calories Burned:
Mindfulness Minutes:

FRIDAY, APRIL 14

Kindness: *Extend and Receive Good Deeds*

HEALTH Watch
Steps Achieved:
Distance Walked:
Calories Burned:
Mindfulness Minutes:

SATURDAY, APRIL 15

Wisdom: *Share Age-Long Experiences*

HEALTH Watch
Steps Achieved:
Distance Walked:
Calories Burned:
Mindfulness Minutes:

SUNDAY, APRIL 16

Spirituality: *Have a Heart Centered Mindset*

HEALTH Watch
Steps Achieved:
Distance Walked:
Calories Burned:
Mindfulness Minutes:

What I learned this week about myself, others, and/or
the world around me:

_____

_____

_____

_____

_____

_____

_____

Exercises that I performed this week:

_____

_____

_____

_____

This week's healthy eating food choices:

_____

_____

_____

_____

APRIL 2023

There are only two ways to live your life. One is as though nothing was a miracle.
The other is as though everything is a miracle.
—Albert Einstein

MONDAY, APRIL 17

Intention: *Focus on Desired Accomplishment*

HEALTH Watch
Steps Achieved:
Distance Walked:
Calories Burned:
Mindfulness Minutes:

TUESDAY, APRIL 18

Gratitude: *Appreciate Everything and Everybody*

HEALTH Watch
Steps Achieved:
Distance Walked:
Calories Burned:
Mindfulness Minutes:

WEDNESDAY, APRIL 19

Affirmation: *Reinforce Self Truth*

HEALTH Watch
Steps Achieved:
Distance Walked:
Calories Burned:
Mindfulness Minutes:

THURSDAY, APRIL 20

Visualization: *Create Your Actuality*

....

....

....

....

....

....

HEALTH Watch
Steps Achieved: ....
Distance Walked: ....
Calories Burned: ....
Mindfulness Minutes: ....

FRIDAY, APRIL 21

Kindness: *Extend and Receive Good Deeds*

....

....

....

....

....

....

HEALTH Watch
Steps Achieved: ....
Distance Walked: ....
Calories Burned: ....
Mindfulness Minutes: ....

SATURDAY, APRIL 22

Wisdom: *Share Age-Long Experiences*

....

....

....

....

....

....

HEALTH Watch
Steps Achieved: ....
Distance Walked: ....
Calories Burned: ....
Mindfulness Minutes: ....

SUNDAY, APRIL 23

Spirituality: *Have a Heart Centered Mindset*

....

....

....

....

....

....

HEALTH Watch
Steps Achieved: ....
Distance Walked: ....
Calories Burned: ....
Mindfulness Minutes: ....

What I learned this week about myself, others, and/or
the world around me:

_____

_____

_____

_____

_____

_____

_____

Exercises that I performed this week:

_____

_____

_____

_____

This week's healthy eating food choices:

_____

_____

_____

_____

APRIL 2023

Nothing is impossible, the word itself says 'I'm possible!'
— Audrey Hepburn

MONDAY, APRIL 24

Intention: *Focus on Desired Accomplishment*

HEALTH Watch
Steps Achieved:
Distance Walked:
Calories Burned:
Mindfulness Minutes:

TUESDAY, APRIL 25

Gratitude: *Appreciate Everything and Everybody*

HEALTH Watch
Steps Achieved:
Distance Walked:
Calories Burned:
Mindfulness Minutes:

WEDNESDAY, APRIL 26

Affirmation: *Reinforce Self Truth*

HEALTH Watch
Steps Achieved:
Distance Walked:
Calories Burned:
Mindfulness Minutes:

THURSDAY, APRIL 27

Visualization: *Create Your Actuality*

HEALTH Watch
Steps Achieved:
Distance Walked:
Calories Burned:
Mindfulness Minutes:

FRIDAY, APRIL 28

Kindness: *Extend and Receive Good Deeds*

HEALTH Watch
Steps Achieved:
Distance Walked:
Calories Burned:
Mindfulness Minutes:

SATURDAY, APRIL 29

Wisdom: *Share Age-Long Experiences*

HEALTH Watch
Steps Achieved:
Distance Walked:
Calories Burned:
Mindfulness Minutes:

SUNDAY, APRIL 30

Spirituality: *Have a Heart Centered Mindset*

HEALTH Watch
Steps Achieved:
Distance Walked:
Calories Burned:
Mindfulness Minutes:

What I learned this week about myself, others, and/or
the world around me:

_____

_____

_____

_____

_____

_____

_____

Exercises that I performed this week:

_____

_____

_____

_____

This week's healthy eating food choices:

_____

_____

_____

_____

MAY 2023

You can never have too many things to look forward to.
—Michael Quigley

MONDAY, MAY 1

Intention: *Focus on Desired Accomplishment*

HEALTH Watch
Steps Achieved:
Distance Walked:
Calories Burned:
Mindfulness Minutes:

TUESDAY, MAY 2

Gratitude: *Appreciate Everything and Everybody*

HEALTH Watch
Steps Achieved:
Distance Walked:
Calories Burned:
Mindfulness Minutes:

WEDNESDAY, MAY 3

Affirmation: *Reinforce Self Truth*

HEALTH Watch
Steps Achieved:
Distance Walked:
Calories Burned:
Mindfulness Minutes:

THURSDAY, MAY 4

Visualization: *Create Your Actuality*

HEALTH Watch	
Steps Achieved:	
Distance Walked:	
Calories Burned:	
Mindfulness Minutes:	

FRIDAY, MAY 5

Kindness: *Extend and Receive Good Deeds*

HEALTH Watch	
Steps Achieved:	
Distance Walked:	
Calories Burned:	
Mindfulness Minutes:	

SATURDAY, MAY 6

Wisdom: *Share Age-Long Experiences*

HEALTH Watch	
Steps Achieved:	
Distance Walked:	
Calories Burned:	
Mindfulness Minutes:	

SUNDAY, MAY 7

Spirituality: *Have a Heart Centered Mindset*

HEALTH Watch	
Steps Achieved:	
Distance Walked:	
Calories Burned:	
Mindfulness Minutes:	

What I learned this week about myself, others, and/or the world around me:

_____

_____

_____

_____

_____

_____

_____

Exercises that I performed this week:

_____

_____

_____

_____

_____

This week's healthy eating food choices:

_____

_____

_____

_____

_____

MAY 2023

Channel your grit and passion.
Follow that small voice inside that makes you come alive.
—Michele Obama

MONDAY, MAY 8

Intention: *Focus on Desired Accomplishment*

HEALTH Watch	
Steps Achieved:	
Distance Walked:	
Calories Burned:	
Mindfulness Minutes:	

TUESDAY, MAY 9

Gratitude: *Appreciate Everything and Everybody*

HEALTH Watch	
Steps Achieved:	
Distance Walked:	
Calories Burned:	
Mindfulness Minutes:	

WEDNESDAY, MAY 10

Affirmation: *Reinforce Self Truth*

HEALTH Watch	
Steps Achieved:	
Distance Walked:	
Calories Burned:	
Mindfulness Minutes:	

THURSDAY, MAY 11

Visualization: *Create Your Actuality*

HEALTH Watch
Steps Achieved:
Distance Walked:
Calories Burned:
Mindfulness Minutes:

FRIDAY, MAY 12

Kindness: *Extend and Receive Good Deeds*

HEALTH Watch
Steps Achieved:
Distance Walked:
Calories Burned:
Mindfulness Minutes:

SATURDAY, MAY 13

Wisdom: *Share Age-Long Experiences*

HEALTH Watch
Steps Achieved:
Distance Walked:
Calories Burned:
Mindfulness Minutes:

SUNDAY, MAY 14

Spirituality: *Have a Heart Centered Mindset*

HEALTH Watch
Steps Achieved:
Distance Walked:
Calories Burned:
Mindfulness Minutes:

What I learned this week about myself, others, and/or
the world around me:

_____

_____

_____

_____

_____

_____

_____

Exercises that I performed this week:

_____

_____

_____

_____

_____

This week's healthy eating food choices:

_____

_____

_____

_____

_____

MAY 2023

Happiness is when what you think, what you say, and what you do are in harmony.
— Mahatma Gandhi

MONDAY, MAY 15

Intention: *Focus on Desired Accomplishment*

HEALTH Watch	
Steps Achieved:	
Distance Walked:	
Calories Burned:	
Mindfulness Minutes:	

TUESDAY, MAY 16

Gratitude: *Appreciate Everything and Everybody*

HEALTH Watch	
Steps Achieved:	
Distance Walked:	
Calories Burned:	
Mindfulness Minutes:	

WEDNESDAY, MAY 17

Affirmation: *Reinforce Self Truth*

HEALTH Watch	
Steps Achieved:	
Distance Walked:	
Calories Burned:	
Mindfulness Minutes:	

THURSDAY, MAY 18

Visualization: *Create Your Actuality*

	HEALTH Watch
	Steps Achieved:
	Distance Walked:
	Calories Burned:
	Mindfulness Minutes:

FRIDAY, MAY 19

Kindness: *Extend and Receive Good Deeds*

	HEALTH Watch
	Steps Achieved:
	Distance Walked:
	Calories Burned:
	Mindfulness Minutes:

SATURDAY, MAY 20

Wisdom: *Share Age-Long Experiences*

	HEALTH Watch
	Steps Achieved:
	Distance Walked:
	Calories Burned:
	Mindfulness Minutes:

SUNDAY, MAY 21

Spirituality: *Have a Heart Centered Mindset*

	HEALTH Watch
	Steps Achieved:
	Distance Walked:
	Calories Burned:
	Mindfulness Minutes:

What I learned this week about myself, others, and/or
the world around me:

....

....

....

....

....

....

....

....

Exercises that I performed this week:

....

....

....

....

This week's healthy eating food choices:

....

....

....

....

MAY 2023

Don't tell people what to do. Offer options. Let them make choices.
They'll feel empowered and confident as a result.

MONDAY, MAY 22

Intention: *Focus on Desired Accomplishment*

	HEALTH Watch
	Steps Achieved:
	Distance Walked:
	Calories Burned:
	Mindfulness Minutes:

TUESDAY, MAY 23

Gratitude: *Appreciate Everything and Everybody*

	HEALTH Watch
	Steps Achieved:
	Distance Walked:
	Calories Burned:
	Mindfulness Minutes:

WEDNESDAY, MAY 24

Affirmation: *Reinforce Self Truth*

	HEALTH Watch
	Steps Achieved:
	Distance Walked:
	Calories Burned:
	Mindfulness Minutes:

THURSDAY, MAY 25

Visualization: *Create Your Actuality*

HEALTH Watch
Steps Achieved:
Distance Walked:
Calories Burned:
Mindfulness Minutes:

FRIDAY, MAY 26

Kindness: *Extend and Receive Good Deeds*

HEALTH Watch
Steps Achieved:
Distance Walked:
Calories Burned:
Mindfulness Minutes:

SATURDAY, MAY 27

Wisdom: *Share Age-Long Experiences*

HEALTH Watch
Steps Achieved:
Distance Walked:
Calories Burned:
Mindfulness Minutes:

SUNDAY, MAY 28

Spirituality: *Have a Heart Centered Mindset*

HEALTH Watch
Steps Achieved:
Distance Walked:
Calories Burned:
Mindfulness Minutes:

What I learned this week about myself, others, and/or
the world around me:

_____

_____

_____

_____

_____

_____

_____

Exercises that I performed this week:

_____

_____

_____

_____

This week's healthy eating food choices:

_____

_____

_____

_____

MAY - JUNE 2023

Heroism doesn't always happen in a burst of glory.
Sometimes small triumphs and large hearts change the course of history.
—Mary Roach

MONDAY, MAY 29

Intention: *Focus on Desired Accomplishment*

HEALTH Watch
Steps Achieved:
Distance Walked:
Calories Burned:
Mindfulness Minutes:

TUESDAY, MAY 30

Gratitude: *Appreciate Everything and Everybody*

HEALTH Watch
Steps Achieved:
Distance Walked:
Calories Burned:
Mindfulness Minutes:

WEDNESDAY, MAY 31

Affirmation: *Reinforce Self Truth*

HEALTH Watch
Steps Achieved:
Distance Walked:
Calories Burned:
Mindfulness Minutes:

THURSDAY, JUNE 1

Visualization: *Create Your Actuality*

	HEALTH Watch
	Steps Achieved:
	Distance Walked:
	Calories Burned:
	Mindfulness Minutes:

FRIDAY, JUNE 2

Kindness: *Extend and Receive Good Deeds*

	HEALTH Watch
	Steps Achieved:
	Distance Walked:
	Calories Burned:
	Mindfulness Minutes:

SATURDAY, JUNE 3

Wisdom: *Share Age-Long Experiences*

	HEALTH Watch
	Steps Achieved:
	Distance Walked:
	Calories Burned:
	Mindfulness Minutes:

SUNDAY, JUNE 4

Spirituality: *Have a Heart Centered Mindset*

	HEALTH Watch
	Steps Achieved:
	Distance Walked:
	Calories Burned:
	Mindfulness Minutes:

What I learned this week about myself, others, and/or
the world around me:

....

....

....

....

....

....

....

Exercises that I performed this week:

....

....

....

....

This week's healthy eating food choices:

....

....

....

....

JUNE 2023

In all great things, the magnificence is in the details.
—Dwaine Canova

MONDAY, JUNE 5

Intention: *Focus on Desired Accomplishment*

HEALTH Watch
Steps Achieved:
Distance Walked:
Calories Burned:
Mindfulness Minutes:

TUESDAY, JUNE 6

Gratitude: *Appreciate Everything and Everybody*

HEALTH Watch
Steps Achieved:
Distance Walked:
Calories Burned:
Mindfulness Minutes:

WEDNESDAY, JUNE 7

Affirmation: *Reinforce Self Truth*

HEALTH Watch
Steps Achieved:
Distance Walked:
Calories Burned:
Mindfulness Minutes:

THURSDAY, JUNE 8

Visualization: *Create Your Actuality*

	HEALTH Watch
	Steps Achieved: ....
	Distance Walked: ....
	Calories Burned: ....
	Mindfulness Minutes: ....

FRIDAY, JUNE 9

Kindness: *Extend and Receive Good Deeds*

	HEALTH Watch
	Steps Achieved: ....
	Distance Walked: ....
	Calories Burned: ....
	Mindfulness Minutes: ....

SATURDAY, JUNE 10

Wisdom: *Share Age-Long Experiences*

	HEALTH Watch
	Steps Achieved: ....
	Distance Walked: ....
	Calories Burned: ....
	Mindfulness Minutes: ....

SUNDAY, JUNE 11

Spirituality: *Have a Heart Centered Mindset*

	HEALTH Watch
	Steps Achieved: ....
	Distance Walked: ....
	Calories Burned: ....
	Mindfulness Minutes: ....

What I learned this week about myself, others, and/or
the world around me:

_____

_____

_____

_____

_____

_____

Exercises that I performed this week:

_____

_____

_____

_____

This week's healthy eating food choices:

_____

_____

_____

_____

JUNE 2023

When you're competent in a world of incompetents, that makes you extraordinary.
—Billy Joel
(August 2022 interview by Fareed Zakaria with Billy Joel on life and what makes one extraordinary)

MONDAY, JUNE 12

Intention: *Focus on Desired Accomplishment*

HEALTH Watch
Steps Achieved: ....
Distance Walked: ....
Calories Burned: ....
Mindfulness Minutes: ....

TUESDAY, JUNE 13

Gratitude: *Appreciate Everything and Everybody*

HEALTH Watch
Steps Achieved: ....
Distance Walked: ....
Calories Burned: ....
Mindfulness Minutes: ....

WEDNESDAY, JUNE 14

Affirmation: *Reinforce Self Truth*

HEALTH Watch
Steps Achieved: ....
Distance Walked: ....
Calories Burned: ....
Mindfulness Minutes: ....

THURSDAY, JUNE 15

Visualization: *Create Your Actuality*

HEALTH Watch
Steps Achieved:
Distance Walked:
Calories Burned:
Mindfulness Minutes:

FRIDAY, JUNE 16

Kindness: *Extend and Receive Good Deeds*

HEALTH Watch
Steps Achieved:
Distance Walked:
Calories Burned:
Mindfulness Minutes:

SATURDAY, JUNE 17

Wisdom: *Share Age-Long Experiences*

HEALTH Watch
Steps Achieved:
Distance Walked:
Calories Burned:
Mindfulness Minutes:

SUNDAY, JUNE 18

Spirituality: *Have a Heart Centered Mindset*

HEALTH Watch
Steps Achieved:
Distance Walked:
Calories Burned:
Mindfulness Minutes:

What I learned this week about myself, others, and/or the world around me:

....

....

....

....

....

....

....

Exercises that I performed this week:

....

....

....

....

....

This week's healthy eating food choices:

....

....

....

....

....

JUNE 2023

You are not what you do.
You are who you were born to be.

MONDAY, JUNE 19

Intention: *Focus on Desired Accomplishment*

	HEALTH Watch
	Steps Achieved:
	Distance Walked:
	Calories Burned:
	Mindfulness Minutes:

TUESDAY, JUNE 20

Gratitude: *Appreciate Everything and Everybody*

	HEALTH Watch
	Steps Achieved:
	Distance Walked:
	Calories Burned:
	Mindfulness Minutes:

WEDNESDAY, JUNE 21

Summer: A time to relax and enjoy nature
Affirmation: *Reinforce Self Truth*

	HEALTH Watch
	Steps Achieved:
	Distance Walked:
	Calories Burned:
	Mindfulness Minutes:

THURSDAY, JUNE 22

Visualization: *Create Your Actuality*

	HEALTH Watch
	Steps Achieved:
	Distance Walked:
	Calories Burned:
	Mindfulness Minutes:

FRIDAY, JUNE 23

Kindness: *Extend and Receive Good Deeds*

	HEALTH Watch
	Steps Achieved:
	Distance Walked:
	Calories Burned:
	Mindfulness Minutes:

SATURDAY, JUNE 24

Wisdom: *Share Age-Long Experiences*

	HEALTH Watch
	Steps Achieved:
	Distance Walked:
	Calories Burned:
	Mindfulness Minutes:

SUNDAY, JUNE 25

Spirituality: *Have a Heart Centered Mindset*

	HEALTH Watch
	Steps Achieved:
	Distance Walked:
	Calories Burned:
	Mindfulness Minutes:

What I learned this week about myself, others, and/or the world around me:

_____

_____

_____

_____

_____

_____

_____

Exercises that I performed this week:

_____

_____

_____

_____

_____

This week's healthy eating food choices:

_____

_____

_____

_____

_____

JUNE – JULY 2023

Do not allow fault-finding negative people to alter your sense of self. You do this by not retaliating and displaying defensive behavior and becoming Fault-finding yourself.

MONDAY, JUNE 26

Intention: *Focus on Desired Accomplishment*

HEALTH Watch
Steps Achieved:
Distance Walked:
Calories Burned:
Mindfulness Minutes:

TUESDAY, JUNE 27

Gratitude: *Appreciate Everything and Everybody*

HEALTH Watch
Steps Achieved:
Distance Walked:
Calories Burned:
Mindfulness Minutes:

WEDNESDAY, JUNE 28

Affirmation: *Reinforce Self Truth*

HEALTH Watch
Steps Achieved:
Distance Walked:
Calories Burned:
Mindfulness Minutes:

THURSDAY, JUNE 29

Visualization: *Create Your Actuality*

HEALTH Watch
Steps Achieved: ....
Distance Walked: ....
Calories Burned: ....
Mindfulness Minutes: ....

FRIDAY, JUNE 30

Kindness: *Extend and Receive Good Deeds*

HEALTH Watch
Steps Achieved: ....
Distance Walked: ....
Calories Burned: ....
Mindfulness Minutes: ....

SATURDAY, JULY 1

Wisdom: *Share Age-Long Experiences*

HEALTH Watch
Steps Achieved: ....
Distance Walked: ....
Calories Burned: ....
Mindfulness Minutes: ....

SUNDAY, JULY 2

Spirituality: *Have a Heart Centered Mindset*

HEALTH Watch
Steps Achieved: ....
Distance Walked: ....
Calories Burned: ....
Mindfulness Minutes: ....

What I learned this week about myself, others, and/or
the world around me:

_____

_____

_____

_____

_____

_____

_____

Exercises that I performed this week:

_____

_____

_____

_____

This week's healthy eating food choices:

_____

_____

_____

_____

JULY 2023

America was not built on fear. America was built on courage,
on imagination, and an unbeatable determination to do the job at hand.
—Harry S. Truman

MONDAY, JULY 3

Intention: *Focus on Desired Accomplishment*

HEALTH Watch	
Steps Achieved:	
Distance Walked:	
Calories Burned:	
Mindfulness Minutes:	

TUESDAY, JULY 4

Gratitude: *Appreciate Everything and Everybody*

HEALTH Watch	
Steps Achieved:	
Distance Walked:	
Calories Burned:	
Mindfulness Minutes:	

WEDNESDAY, JULY 5

Affirmation: *Reinforce Self Truth*

HEALTH Watch	
Steps Achieved:	
Distance Walked:	
Calories Burned:	
Mindfulness Minutes:	

THURSDAY, JULY 6

Visualization: *Create Your Actuality*

....
....
....
....
....
....

Steps Achieved: ....

Distance Walked: ....

Calories Burned: ....

Mindfulness Minutes: ....

FRIDAY, JULY 7

Kindness: *Extend and Receive Good Deeds*

....
....
....
....
....
....

HEALTH Watch

Steps Achieved: ....

Distance Walked: ....

Calories Burned: ....

Mindfulness Minutes: ....

SATURDAY, JULY 8

Wisdom: *Share Age-Long Experiences*

....
....
....
....
....
....

HEALTH Watch

Steps Achieved: ....

Distance Walked: ....

Calories Burned: ....

Mindfulness Minutes: ....

SUNDAY, JULY 9

Spirituality: *Have a Heart Centered Mindset*

....
....
....
....
....
....

HEALTH Watch

Steps Achieved: ....

Distance Walked: ....

Calories Burned: ....

Mindfulness Minutes: ....

What I learned this week about myself, others, and/or the world around me:

....

....

....

....

....

....

....

Exercises that I performed this week:

....

....

....

....

This week's healthy eating food choices:

....

....

....

....

JULY 2023

Honor the Past; Celebrate the Present;
Build the Future

MONDAY, JULY 10

Intention: *Focus on Desired Accomplishment*

	HEALTH Watch
....	Steps Achieved: ....
....	Distance Walked: ....
....	Calories Burned: ....
....	Mindfulness Minutes: ....

TUESDAY, JULY 11

Gratitude: *Appreciate Everything and Everybody*

	HEALTH Watch
....	Steps Achieved: ....
....	Distance Walked: ....
....	Calories Burned: ....
....	Mindfulness Minutes: ....

WEDNESDAY, JULY 12

Affirmation: *Reinforce Self Truth*

	HEALTH Watch
....	Steps Achieved: ....
....	Distance Walked: ....
....	Calories Burned: ....
....	Mindfulness Minutes: ....

THURSDAY, JULY 13

Visualization: *Create Your Actuality*

....

HEALTH Watch
Steps Achieved: ....
Distance Walked: ....
Calories Burned: ....
Mindfulness Minutes: ....

FRIDAY, JULY 14

Kindness: *Extend and Receive Good Deeds*

....

HEALTH Watch
Steps Achieved: ....
Distance Walked: ....
Calories Burned: ....
Mindfulness Minutes: ....

SATURDAY, JULY 15

Wisdom: *Share Age-Long Experiences*

....

HEALTH Watch
Steps Achieved: ....
Distance Walked: ....
Calories Burned: ....
Mindfulness Minutes: ....

SUNDAY, JULY 16

Spirituality: *Have a Heart Centered Mindset*

....

HEALTH Watch
Steps Achieved: ....
Distance Walked: ....
Calories Burned: ....
Mindfulness Minutes: ....

What I learned this week about myself, others, and/or the world around me:

_____
_____
_____
_____
_____
_____
_____

Exercises that I performed this week:

_____
_____
_____
_____

This week's healthy eating food choices:

_____
_____
_____
_____

JULY 2023

It's not your fault you got knocked down; it is your responsibility to get back up.
—Joel Osteen

MONDAY, JULY 17

Intention: *Focus on Desired Accomplishment*

HEALTH Watch
Steps Achieved: ....
Distance Walked: ....
Calories Burned: ....
Mindfulness Minutes: ....

TUESDAY, JULY 18

Gratitude: *Appreciate Everything and Everybody*

HEALTH Watch
Steps Achieved: ....
Distance Walked: ....
Calories Burned: ....
Mindfulness Minutes: ....

WEDNESDAY, JULY 19

Affirmation: *Reinforce Self Truth*

HEALTH Watch
Steps Achieved: ....
Distance Walked: ....
Calories Burned: ....
Mindfulness Minutes: ....

THURSDAY, JULY 20

Visualization: *Create Your Actuality*

HEALTH Watch
Steps Achieved: ....
Distance Walked: ....
Calories Burned: ....
Mindfulness Minutes: ....

FRIDAY, JULY 21

Kindness: *Extend and Receive Good Deeds*

HEALTH Watch
Steps Achieved: ....
Distance Walked: ....
Calories Burned: ....
Mindfulness Minutes: ....

SATURDAY, JULY 22

Wisdom: *Share Age-Long Experiences*

HEALTH Watch
Steps Achieved: ....
Distance Walked: ....
Calories Burned: ....
Mindfulness Minutes: ....

SUNDAY, JULY 23

Spirituality: *Have a Heart Centered Mindset*

HEALTH Watch
Steps Achieved: ....
Distance Walked: ....
Calories Burned: ....
Mindfulness Minutes: ....

What I learned this week about myself, others, and/or
the world around me:

_____

_____

_____

_____

_____

_____

_____

Exercises that I performed this week:

_____

_____

_____

_____

This week's healthy eating food choices:

_____

_____

_____

_____

JULY 2023

Faith is believing in what you can't see.
Compassion produces great results than criticism or blame.

MONDAY, JULY 24

Intention: *Focus on Desired Accomplishment*

HEALTH Watch
Steps Achieved: ....
Distance Walked: ....
Calories Burned: ....
Mindfulness Minutes: ....

TUESDAY, JULY 25

Gratitude: *Appreciate Everything and Everybody*

HEALTH Watch
Steps Achieved: ....
Distance Walked: ....
Calories Burned: ....
Mindfulness Minutes: ....

WEDNESDAY, JULY 26

Affirmation: *Reinforce Self Truth*

HEALTH Watch
Steps Achieved: ....
Distance Walked: ....
Calories Burned: ....
Mindfulness Minutes: ....

THURSDAY, JULY 27

Visualization: *Create Your Actuality*

	HEALTH Watch
	Steps Achieved: ....
	Distance Walked: ....
	Calories Burned: ....
	Mindfulness Minutes: ....

FRIDAY, JULY 28

Kindness: *Extend and Receive Good Deeds*

	HEALTH Watch
	Steps Achieved: ....
	Distance Walked: ....
	Calories Burned: ....
	Mindfulness Minutes: ....

SATURDAY, JULY 29

Wisdom: *Share Age-Long Experiences*

	HEALTH Watch
	Steps Achieved: ....
	Distance Walked: ....
	Calories Burned: ....
	Mindfulness Minutes: ....

SUNDAY, JULY 30

Spirituality: *Have a Heart Centered Mindset*

	HEALTH Watch
	Steps Achieved: ....
	Distance Walked: ....
	Calories Burned: ....
	Mindfulness Minutes: ....

What I learned this week about myself, others, and/or
the world around me:

_____

_____

_____

_____

_____

_____

Exercises that I performed this week:

_____

_____

_____

_____

This week's healthy eating food choices:

_____

_____

_____

_____

JULY - AUGUST 2023

My heart is my unwavering guide.
The joy I like to share is borne from that sacred relationship.
—Erica Hervol

MONDAY, JULY 31

Intention: *Focus on Desired Accomplishment*

HEALTH Watch
Steps Achieved:
Distance Walked:
Calories Burned:
Mindfulness Minutes:

TUESDAY, AUGUST 1

Gratitude: *Appreciate Everything and Everybody*

HEALTH Watch
Steps Achieved:
Distance Walked:
Calories Burned:
Mindfulness Minutes:

WEDNESDAY, *AUGUST 2*

Affirmation: *Reinforce Self Truth*

HEALTH Watch
Steps Achieved:
Distance Walked:
Calories Burned:
Mindfulness Minutes:

THURSDAY, AUGUST 3

Visualization: *Create Your Actuality*

HEALTH Watch
Steps Achieved:
Distance Walked:
Calories Burned:
Mindfulness Minutes:

FRIDAY, *AUGUST 4*

Kindness: *Extend and Receive Good Deeds*

HEALTH Watch
Steps Achieved:
Distance Walked:
Calories Burned:
Mindfulness Minutes:

SATURDAY, *AUGUST 5*

Wisdom: *Share Age-Long Experiences*

HEALTH Watch
Steps Achieved:
Distance Walked:
Calories Burned:
Mindfulness Minutes:

SUNDAY, *AUGUST 6*

Spirituality: *Have a Heart Centered Mindset*

HEALTH Watch
Steps Achieved:
Distance Walked:
Calories Burned:
Mindfulness Minutes:

What I learned this week about myself, others, and/or the world around me:

_____

_____

_____

_____

_____

_____

_____

Exercises that I performed this week:

_____

_____

_____

_____

This week's healthy eating food choices:

_____

_____

_____

_____

AUGUST 2023

The difference between hearing and listening is comprehension;
The difference between knowledge and wisdom is experience.
—Lon Safko

MONDAY, AUGUST 7

Intention: *Focus on Desired Accomplishment*

HEALTH Watch
Steps Achieved: ....
Distance Walked: ....
Calories Burned: ....
Mindfulness Minutes: ....

TUESDAY, AUGUST 8

Gratitude: *Appreciate Everything and Everybody*

HEALTH Watch
Steps Achieved: ....
Distance Walked: ....
Calories Burned: ....
Mindfulness Minutes: ....

WEDNESDAY, AUGUST 9

Affirmation: *Reinforce Self Truth*

HEALTH Watch
Steps Achieved: ....
Distance Walked: ....
Calories Burned: ....
Mindfulness Minutes: ....

THURSDAY, AUGUST 10

Visualization: *Create Your Actuality*

....

HEALTH Watch
Steps Achieved: ....
Distance Walked: ....
Calories Burned: ....
Mindfulness Minutes: ....

FRIDAY, AUGUST 11

Kindness: *Extend and Receive Good Deeds*

....

HEALTH Watch
Steps Achieved: ....
Distance Walked: ....
Calories Burned: ....
Mindfulness Minutes: ....

SATURDAY, AUGUST 12

Wisdom: *Share Age-Long Experiences*

....

HEALTH Watch
Steps Achieved: ....
Distance Walked: ....
Calories Burned: ....
Mindfulness Minutes: ....

SUNDAY, AUGUST 13

Spirituality: *Have a Heart Centered Mindset*

....

HEALTH Watch
Steps Achieved: ....
Distance Walked: ....
Calories Burned: ....
Mindfulness Minutes: ....

What I learned this week about myself, others, and/or the world around me:

_____

_____

_____

_____

_____

_____

_____

Exercises that I performed this week:

_____

_____

_____

_____

This week's healthy eating food choices:

_____

_____

_____

_____

AUGUST 2023

No one can make you feel inferior without your consent.
—Eleanor Roosevelt

MONDAY, AUGUST 14

Intention: *Focus on Desired Accomplishment*

HEALTH Watch
Steps Achieved:
Distance Walked:
Calories Burned:
Mindfulness Minutes:

TUESDAY, AUGUST 15

Gratitude: *Appreciate Everything and Everybody*

HEALTH Watch
Steps Achieved:
Distance Walked:
Calories Burned:
Mindfulness Minutes:

WEDNESDAY, AUGUST 16

Affirmation: *Reinforce Self Truth*

HEALTH Watch
Steps Achieved:
Distance Walked:
Calories Burned:
Mindfulness Minutes:

THURSDAY, AUGUST 17

Visualization: *Create Your Actuality*

HEALTH Watch
Steps Achieved:
Distance Walked:
Calories Burned:
Mindfulness Minutes:

FRIDAY, AUGUST 18

Kindness: *Extend and Receive Good Deeds*

HEALTH Watch
Steps Achieved:
Distance Walked:
Calories Burned:
Mindfulness Minutes:

SATURDAY, AUGUST 19

Wisdom: *Share Age-Long Experiences*

HEALTH Watch
Steps Achieved:
Distance Walked:
Calories Burned:
Mindfulness Minutes:

SUNDAY, AUGUST 20

Spirituality: *Have a Heart Centered Mindset*

HEALTH Watch
Steps Achieved:
Distance Walked:
Calories Burned:
Mindfulness Minutes:

What I learned this week about myself, others, and/or the world around me:

_____

_____

_____

_____

_____

_____

_____

Exercises that I performed this week:

_____

_____

_____

_____

This week's healthy eating food choices:

_____

_____

_____

_____

AUGUST 2023

Appreciate people who are not just like you.
When disagreeing, be understanding—not judgmental.

MONDAY, AUGUST 21

Intention: *Focus on Desired Accomplishment*

HEALTH Watch
Steps Achieved:
Distance Walked:
Calories Burned:
Mindfulness Minutes:

TUESDAY, AUGUST 22

Gratitude: *Appreciate Everything and Everybody*

HEALTH Watch
Steps Achieved:
Distance Walked:
Calories Burned:
Mindfulness Minutes:

WEDNESDAY, AUGUST 23

Affirmation: *Reinforce Self Truth*

HEALTH Watch
Steps Achieved:
Distance Walked:
Calories Burned:
Mindfulness Minutes:

THURSDAY, AUGUST 24

Visualization: *Create Your Actuality*

HEALTH Watch
Steps Achieved: ....
Distance Walked: ....
Calories Burned: ....
Mindfulness Minutes: ....

FRIDAY, AUGUST 25

Kindness: *Extend and Receive Good Deeds*

HEALTH Watch
Steps Achieved: ....
Distance Walked: ....
Calories Burned: ....
Mindfulness Minutes: ....

SATURDAY, AUGUST 26

Wisdom: *Share Age-Long Experiences*

HEALTH Watch
Steps Achieved: ....
Distance Walked: ....
Calories Burned: ....
Mindfulness Minutes: ....

SUNDAY, AUGUST 27

Spirituality: *Have a Heart Centered Mindset*

HEALTH Watch
Steps Achieved: ....
Distance Walked: ....
Calories Burned: ....
Mindfulness Minutes: ....

What I learned this week about myself, others, and/or the world around me:

....
....
....
....
....
....
....
....

Exercises that I performed this week:

....
....
....
....
....

This week's healthy eating food choices:

....
....
....
....
....

AUGUST – SEPTEMBER 2023

*Don't let the tension build into an explosion. Instead, hit the control button.
Someone has got to be in control. Let it be You!*

MONDAY, AUGUST 28

Intention: *Focus on Desired Accomplishment*

HEALTH Watch
Steps Achieved: ....
Distance Walked: ....
Calories Burned: ....
Mindfulness Minutes: ....

TUESDAY, AUGUST 29

Gratitude: *Appreciate Everything and Everybody*

HEALTH Watch
Steps Achieved: ....
Distance Walked: ....
Calories Burned: ....
Mindfulness Minutes: ....

WEDNESDAY, AUGUST 30

Affirmation: *Reinforce Self Truth*

HEALTH Watch
Steps Achieved: ....
Distance Walked: ....
Calories Burned: ....
Mindfulness Minutes: ....

THURSDAY, AUGUST 31

Visualization: *Create Your Actuality*

HEALTH Watch
Steps Achieved: ....
Distance Walked: ....
Calories Burned: ....
Mindfulness Minutes: ....

FRIDAY, SEPTEMBER 1

Kindness: *Extend and Receive Good Deeds*

HEALTH Watch
Steps Achieved: ....
Distance Walked: ....
Calories Burned: ....
Mindfulness Minutes: ....

SATURDAY, SEPTEMBER 2

Wisdom: *Share Age-Long Experiences*

HEALTH Watch
Steps Achieved: ....
Distance Walked: ....
Calories Burned: ....
Mindfulness Minutes: ....

SUNDAY, SEPTEMBER 3

Spirituality: *Have a Heart Centered Mindset*

HEALTH Watch
Steps Achieved: ....
Distance Walked: ....
Calories Burned: ....
Mindfulness Minutes: ....

What I learned this week about myself, others, and/or
the world around me:

_____

_____

_____

_____

_____

_____

_____

Exercises that I performed this week:

_____

_____

_____

_____

This week's healthy eating food choices:

_____

_____

_____

_____

SEPTEMBER 2023

Happiness comes from my expectation.
—' Prof' Roberto Ancis

MONDAY, SEPTEMBER 4

Intention: *Focus on Desired Accomplishment*

HEALTH Watch
Steps Achieved:
Distance Walked:
Calories Burned:
Mindfulness Minutes:

TUESDAY, SEPTEMBER 5

Gratitude: *Appreciate Everything and Everybody*

HEALTH Watch
Steps Achieved:
Distance Walked:
Calories Burned:
Mindfulness Minutes:

WEDNESDAY, SEPTEMBER 6

Affirmation: *Reinforce Self Truth*

HEALTH Watch
Steps Achieved:
Distance Walked:
Calories Burned:
Mindfulness Minutes:

THURSDAY, SEPTEMBER 7

Visualization: *Create Your Actuality*

HEALTH Watch
Steps Achieved:
Distance Walked:
Calories Burned:
Mindfulness Minutes:

FRIDAY, SEPTEMBER 8

Kindness: *Extend and Receive Good Deeds*

HEALTH Watch
Steps Achieved:
Distance Walked:
Calories Burned:
Mindfulness Minutes:

SATURDAY, SEPTEMBER 9

Wisdom: *Share Age-Long Experiences*

HEALTH Watch
Steps Achieved:
Distance Walked:
Calories Burned:
Mindfulness Minutes:

SUNDAY, SEPTEMBER 10

Spirituality: *Have a Heart Centered Mindset*

HEALTH Watch
Steps Achieved:
Distance Walked:
Calories Burned:
Mindfulness Minutes:

What I learned this week about myself, others, and/or the world around me:

_____

_____

_____

_____

_____

_____

Exercises that I performed this week:

_____

_____

_____

_____

This week's healthy eating food choices:

_____

_____

_____

_____

SEPTEMBER 2023

Rest when you're weary. Refresh and renew yourself, your body, your mind, and your spirit. Then get back to work.
—Ralph Marston

MONDAY, SEPTEMBER 11

Intention: *Focus on Desired Accomplishment*

HEALTH Watch
Steps Achieved: ....
Distance Walked: ....
Calories Burned: ....
Mindfulness Minutes: ....

TUESDAY, SEPTEMBER 12

Gratitude: *Appreciate Everything and Everybody*

HEALTH Watch
Steps Achieved: ....
Distance Walked: ....
Calories Burned: ....
Mindfulness Minutes: ....

WEDNESDAY, SEPTEMBER 13

Affirmation: *Reinforce Self Truth*

HEALTH Watch
Steps Achieved: ....
Distance Walked: ....
Calories Burned: ....
Mindfulness Minutes: ....

THURSDAY, SEPTEMBER 14

Visualization: *Create Your Actuality*

....
....
....
....
....
....

HEALTH Watch
Steps Achieved: ....
Distance Walked: ....
Calories Burned: ....
Mindfulness Minutes: ....

FRIDAY, SEPTEMBER 15

Kindness: *Extend and Receive Good Deeds*

....
....
....
....
....
....

HEALTH Watch
Steps Achieved: ....
Distance Walked: ....
Calories Burned: ....
Mindfulness Minutes: ....

SATURDAY, SEPTEMBER 16

Wisdom: *Share Age-Long Experiences*

....
....
....
....
....
....

HEALTH Watch
Steps Achieved: ....
Distance Walked: ....
Calories Burned: ....
Mindfulness Minutes: ....

SUNDAY, SEPTEMBER 17

Spirituality: *Have a Heart Centered Mindset*

....
....
....
....
....
....

HEALTH Watch
Steps Achieved: ....
Distance Walked: ....
Calories Burned: ....
Mindfulness Minutes: ....

What I learned this week about myself, others, and/or the world around me:

_____

_____

_____

_____

_____

_____

_____

Exercises that I performed this week:

_____

_____

_____

_____

This week's healthy eating food choices:

_____

_____

_____

_____

SEPTEMBER 2023

*When troubled or faced with adversity, keep the faith, have hope,
and look for better days to come.*

MONDAY, SEPTEMBER 18

Intention: *Focus on Desired Accomplishment*

HEALTH Watch
Steps Achieved: ....
Distance Walked: ....
Calories Burned: ....
Mindfulness Minutes: ....

TUESDAY, SEPTEMBER 19

Gratitude: *Appreciate Everything and Everybody*

HEALTH Watch
Steps Achieved: ....
Distance Walked: ....
Calories Burned: ....
Mindfulness Minutes: ....

WEDNESDAY, SEPTEMBER 20

Affirmation: *Reinforce Self Truth*

HEALTH Watch
Steps Achieved: ....
Distance Walked: ....
Calories Burned: ....
Mindfulness Minutes: ....

THURSDAY, SEPTEMBER 21

Fall: A time of letting go

Visualization: *Create Your Actuality*

HEALTH Watch
Steps Achieved:
Distance Walked:
Calories Burned:
Mindfulness Minutes:

FRIDAY, SEPTEMBER 22

Kindness: *Extend and Receive Good Deeds*

HEALTH Watch
Steps Achieved:
Distance Walked:
Calories Burned:
Mindfulness Minutes:

SATURDAY, SEPTEMBER 23

Wisdom: *Share Age-Long Experiences*

HEALTH Watch
Steps Achieved:
Distance Walked:
Calories Burned:
Mindfulness Minutes:

SUNDAY, SEPTEMBER 24

Spirituality: *Have a Heart Centered Mindset*

HEALTH Watch
Steps Achieved:
Distance Walked:
Calories Burned:
Mindfulness Minutes:

What I learned this week about myself, others, and/or the world around me:

_____

_____

_____

_____

_____

_____

_____

Exercises that I performed this week:

_____

_____

_____

_____

This week's healthy eating food choices:

_____

_____

_____

_____

SEPTEMBER – OCTOBER 2023

Having a difficult day? Recalibrate!
A new day equals a fresh beginning.

MONDAY, SEPTEMBER 25

Intention: *Focus on Desired Accomplishment*

HEALTH Watch
Steps Achieved:
Distance Walked:
Calories Burned:
Mindfulness Minutes:

TUESDAY, SEPTEMBER 26

Gratitude: *Appreciate Everything and Everybody*

HEALTH Watch
Steps Achieved:
Distance Walked:
Calories Burned:
Mindfulness Minutes:

WEDNESDAY, SEPTEMBER 27

Affirmation: *Reinforce Self Truth*

HEALTH Watch
Steps Achieved:
Distance Walked:
Calories Burned:
Mindfulness Minutes:

THURSDAY, SEPTEMBER 28

Visualization: *Create Your Actuality*

....
....
....
....
....

HEALTH Watch
Steps Achieved: ....
Distance Walked: ....
Calories Burned: ....
Mindfulness Minutes: ....

FRIDAY, SEPTEMBER 29

Kindness: *Extend and Receive Good Deeds*

....
....
....
....
....

HEALTH Watch
Steps Achieved: ....
Distance Walked: ....
Calories Burned: ....
Mindfulness Minutes: ....

SATURDAY, SEPTEMBER 30

Wisdom: *Share Age-Long Experiences*

....
....
....
....
....

HEALTH Watch
Steps Achieved: ....
Distance Walked: ....
Calories Burned: ....
Mindfulness Minutes: ....

SUNDAY, OCTOBER 1

Spirituality: *Have a Heart Centered Mindset*

....
....
....
....
....

HEALTH Watch
Steps Achieved: ....
Distance Walked: ....
Calories Burned: ....
Mindfulness Minutes: ....

What I learned this week about myself, others, and/or the world around me:

_____

_____

_____

_____

_____

_____

_____

Exercises that I performed this week:

_____

_____

_____

_____

This week's healthy eating food choices:

_____

_____

_____

_____

OCTOBER 2023

Some doings of Man, in certain crucial moments of Mankind, the inexorable march of time will not dismiss. Be mindful of what you can do for positive change today.
—Vlady Cornateanu

MONDAY, OCTOBER 2

Intention: *Focus on Desired Accomplishment*

HEALTH Watch
Steps Achieved:
Distance Walked:
Calories Burned:
Mindfulness Minutes:

TUESDAY, OCTOBER 3

Gratitude: *Appreciate Everything and Everybody*

HEALTH Watch
Steps Achieved:
Distance Walked:
Calories Burned:
Mindfulness Minutes:

WEDNESDAY, OCTOBER 4

Affirmation: *Reinforce Self Truth*

HEALTH Watch
Steps Achieved:
Distance Walked:
Calories Burned:
Mindfulness Minutes:

THURSDAY, OCTOBER 5

Visualization: *Create Your Actuality*

HEALTH Watch
Steps Achieved:
Distance Walked:
Calories Burned:
Mindfulness Minutes:

FRIDAY, OCTOBER 6

Kindness: *Extend and Receive Good Deeds*

HEALTH Watch
Steps Achieved:
Distance Walked:
Calories Burned:
Mindfulness Minutes:

SATURDAY, OCTOBER 7

Wisdom: *Share Age-Long Experiences*

HEALTH Watch
Steps Achieved:
Distance Walked:
Calories Burned:
Mindfulness Minutes:

SUNDAY, OCTOBER 8

Spirituality: *Have a Heart Centered Mindset*

HEALTH Watch
Steps Achieved:
Distance Walked:
Calories Burned:
Mindfulness Minutes:

What I learned this week about myself, others, and/or the world around me:

....

....

....

....

....

....

....

Exercises that I performed this week:

....

....

....

....

....

This week's healthy eating food choices:

....

....

....

....

....

OCTOBER 2023

Goals are simply tools to focus your energy in positive directions,
these can be changed as your priorities change, new ones added, and others dropped.
—Christopher Columbus

MONDAY, OCTOBER 9

Intention: *Focus on Desired Accomplishment*

HEALTH Watch
Steps Achieved:
Distance Walked:
Calories Burned:
Mindfulness Minutes:

TUESDAY, OCTOBER 10

Gratitude: *Appreciate Everything and Everybody*

HEALTH Watch
Steps Achieved:
Distance Walked:
Calories Burned:
Mindfulness Minutes:

WEDNESDAY, OCTOBER 11

Affirmation: *Reinforce Self Truth*

HEALTH Watch
Steps Achieved:
Distance Walked:
Calories Burned:
Mindfulness Minutes:

THURSDAY, OCTOBER 12

Visualization: *Create Your Actuality*

HEALTH Watch
Steps Achieved: ....
Distance Walked: ....
Calories Burned: ....
Mindfulness Minutes: ....

FRIDAY, OCTOBER 13

Kindness: *Extend and Receive Good Deeds*

HEALTH Watch
Steps Achieved: ....
Distance Walked: ....
Calories Burned: ....
Mindfulness Minutes: ....

SATURDAY, OCTOBER 14

Wisdom: *Share Age-Long Experiences*

HEALTH Watch
Steps Achieved: ....
Distance Walked: ....
Calories Burned: ....
Mindfulness Minutes: ....

SUNDAY, OCTOBER 15

Spirituality: *Have a Heart Centered Mindset*

HEALTH Watch
Steps Achieved: ....
Distance Walked: ....
Calories Burned: ....
Mindfulness Minutes: ....

What I learned this week about myself, others, and/or
the world around me:

_____

_____

_____

_____

_____

_____

_____

Exercises that I performed this week:

_____

_____

_____

_____

_____

This week's healthy eating food choices:

_____

_____

_____

_____

OCTOBER 2023

Only through experience of trial and suffering can the soul be strengthened, vision cleared, ambition inspired, and success achieved.
— Helen Keller

MONDAY, OCTOBER 16

Intention: *Focus on Desired Accomplishment*

HEALTH Watch
Steps Achieved:
Distance Walked:
Calories Burned:
Mindfulness Minutes:

TUESDAY, OCTOBER 17

Gratitude: *Appreciate Everything and Everybody*

HEALTH Watch
Steps Achieved:
Distance Walked:
Calories Burned:
Mindfulness Minutes:

WEDNESDAY, OCTOBER 18

Affirmation: *Reinforce Self Truth*

HEALTH Watch
Steps Achieved:
Distance Walked:
Calories Burned:
Mindfulness Minutes:

THURSDAY, OCTOBER 19

Visualization: *Create Your Actuality*

HEALTH Watch
Steps Achieved:
Distance Walked:
Calories Burned:
Mindfulness Minutes:

FRIDAY, OCTOBER 20

Kindness: *Extend and Receive Good Deeds*

HEALTH Watch
Steps Achieved:
Distance Walked:
Calories Burned:
Mindfulness Minutes:

SATURDAY, OCTOBER 21

Wisdom: *Share Age-Long Experiences*

HEALTH Watch
Steps Achieved:
Distance Walked:
Calories Burned:
Mindfulness Minutes:

SUNDAY, OCTOBER 22

Spirituality: *Have a Heart Centered Mindset*

HEALTH Watch
Steps Achieved:
Distance Walked:
Calories Burned:
Mindfulness Minutes:

What I learned this week about myself, others, and/or
the world around me:

_____

_____

_____

_____

_____

_____

_____

_____

Exercises that I performed this week:

_____

_____

_____

_____

_____

This week's healthy eating food choices:

_____

_____

_____

_____

OCTOBER 2023

Everyone has special gifts or talents. Find yours and use them.
You may find gifts in areas you might not have guessed.

MONDAY, OCTOBER 23

Intention: *Focus on Desired Accomplishment*

HEALTH Watch
Steps Achieved:
Distance Walked:
Calories Burned:
Mindfulness Minutes:

TUESDAY, OCTOBER 24

Gratitude: *Appreciate Everything and Everybody*

HEALTH Watch
Steps Achieved:
Distance Walked:
Calories Burned:
Mindfulness Minutes:

WEDNESDAY, OCTOBER 25

Affirmation: *Reinforce Self Truth*

HEALTH Watch
Steps Achieved:
Distance Walked:
Calories Burned:
Mindfulness Minutes:

THURSDAY, OCTOBER 26

Visualization: *Create Your Actuality*

HEALTH Watch
Steps Achieved:
Distance Walked:
Calories Burned:
Mindfulness Minutes:

FRIDAY, OCTOBER 27

Kindness: *Extend and Receive Good Deeds*

HEALTH Watch
Steps Achieved:
Distance Walked:
Calories Burned:
Mindfulness Minutes:

SATURDAY, OCTOBER 28

Wisdom: *Share Age-Long Experiences*

HEALTH Watch
Steps Achieved:
Distance Walked:
Calories Burned:
Mindfulness Minutes:

SUNDAY, OCTOBER 29

Spirituality: *Have a Heart Centered Mindset*

HEALTH Watch
Steps Achieved:
Distance Walked:
Calories Burned:
Mindfulness Minutes:

What I learned this week about myself, others, and/or the world around me:

_____

_____

_____

_____

_____

_____

_____

Exercises that I performed this week:

_____

_____

_____

_____

This week's healthy eating food choices:

_____

_____

_____

_____

OCTOBER – NOVEMBER 2023

When you stop, you see; when you see, you listen;
when you listen, you act.

MONDAY, OCTOBER 30

Intention: *Focus on Desired Accomplishment*

HEALTH Watch
Steps Achieved: ....
Distance Walked: ....
Calories Burned: ....
Mindfulness Minutes: ....

TUESDAY, OCTOBER 31

Gratitude: *Appreciate Everything and Everybody*

HEALTH Watch
Steps Achieved: ....
Distance Walked: ....
Calories Burned: ....
Mindfulness Minutes: ....

WEDNESDAY, NOVEMBER 1

Affirmation: *Reinforce Self Truth*

HEALTH Watch
Steps Achieved: ....
Distance Walked: ....
Calories Burned: ....
Mindfulness Minutes: ....

THURSDAY, NOVEMBER 2

Visualization: *Create Your Actuality*

HEALTH Watch
Steps Achieved: ....
Distance Walked: ....
Calories Burned: ....
Mindfulness Minutes: ....

FRIDAY, NOVEMBER 3

Kindness: *Extend and Receive Good Deeds*

HEALTH Watch
Steps Achieved: ....
Distance Walked: ....
Calories Burned: ....
Mindfulness Minutes: ....

SATURDAY, NOVEMBER 4

Wisdom: *Share Age-Long Experiences*

HEALTH Watch
Steps Achieved: ....
Distance Walked: ....
Calories Burned: ....
Mindfulness Minutes: ....

SUNDAY, NOVEMBER 5

Spirituality: *Have a Heart Centered Mindset*

HEALTH Watch
Steps Achieved: ....
Distance Walked: ....
Calories Burned: ....
Mindfulness Minutes: ....

What I learned this week about myself, others, and/or
the world around me:

_____

_____

_____

_____

_____

_____

_____

Exercises that I performed this week:

_____

_____

_____

_____

This week's healthy eating food choices:

_____

_____

_____

_____

NOVEMBER 2023

A hero is someone who has given his or her life to something bigger than oneself.
—Joseph Campbell

MONDAY, NOVEMBER 6

Intention: *Focus on Desired Accomplishment*

HEALTH Watch
Steps Achieved: ....
Distance Walked: ....
Calories Burned: ....
Mindfulness Minutes: ....

TUESDAY, NOVEMBER 7

Gratitude: *Appreciate Everything and Everybody*

HEALTH Watch
Steps Achieved: ....
Distance Walked: ....
Calories Burned: ....
Mindfulness Minutes: ....

WEDNESDAY, NOVEMBER 8

Affirmation: *Reinforce Self Truth*

HEALTH Watch
Steps Achieved: ....
Distance Walked: ....
Calories Burned: ....
Mindfulness Minutes: ....

THURSDAY, NOVEMBER 9

Visualization: *Create Your Actuality*

HEALTH Watch

Steps Achieved: ....

Distance Walked: ....

Calories Burned: ....

Mindfulness Minutes: ....

FRIDAY, NOVEMBER 10

Kindness: *Extend and Receive Good Deeds*

HEALTH Watch

Steps Achieved: ....

Distance Walked: ....

Calories Burned: ....

Mindfulness Minutes: ....

SATURDAY, NOVEMBER 11

Wisdom: *Share Age-Long Experiences*

HEALTH Watch

Steps Achieved: ....

Distance Walked: ....

Calories Burned: ....

Mindfulness Minutes: ....

SUNDAY, NOVEMBER 12

Spirituality: *Have a Heart Centered Mindset*

HEALTH Watch

Steps Achieved: ....

Distance Walked: ....

Calories Burned: ....

Mindfulness Minutes: ....

What I learned this week about myself, others, and/or
the world around me:

_____

_____

_____

_____

_____

_____

_____

Exercises that I performed this week:

_____

_____

_____

_____

This week's healthy eating food choices:

_____

_____

_____

_____

NOVEMBER 2023

To become a better you, remember to be grateful to people who have contributed to making you who you are today.
— Israelmore Ayivor

MONDAY, NOVEMBER 13

Intention: *Focus on Desired Accomplishment*

HEALTH Watch
Steps Achieved:
Distance Walked:
Calories Burned:
Mindfulness Minutes:

TUESDAY, NOVEMBER 14

Gratitude: *Appreciate Everything and Everybody*

HEALTH Watch
Steps Achieved:
Distance Walked:
Calories Burned:
Mindfulness Minutes:

WEDNESDAY, NOVEMBER 15

Affirmation: *Reinforce Self Truth*

HEALTH Watch
Steps Achieved:
Distance Walked:
Calories Burned:
Mindfulness Minutes:

THURSDAY, NOVEMBER 16

Visualization: *Create Your Actuality*

HEALTH Watch
Steps Achieved:
Distance Walked:
Calories Burned:
Mindfulness Minutes:

FRIDAY, NOVEMBER 17

Kindness: *Extend and Receive Good Deeds*

HEALTH Watch
Steps Achieved:
Distance Walked:
Calories Burned:
Mindfulness Minutes:

SATURDAY, NOVEMBER 18

Wisdom: *Share Age-Long Experiences*

HEALTH Watch
Steps Achieved:
Distance Walked:
Calories Burned:
Mindfulness Minutes:

SUNDAY, NOVEMBER 19

Spirituality: *Have a Heart Centered Mindset*

HEALTH Watch
Steps Achieved:
Distance Walked:
Calories Burned:
Mindfulness Minutes:

What I learned this week about myself, others, and/or
the world around me:

_____

_____

_____

_____

_____

_____

_____

Exercises that I performed this week:

_____

_____

_____

_____

This week's healthy eating food choices:

_____

_____

_____

_____

NOVEMBER 2023

*No matter what the situation is...close your eyes and
think of all the things in your life you could be grateful for right now.*
—Deepak Chopra

MONDAY, NOVEMBER 20

Intention: *Focus on Desired Accomplishment*

HEALTH Watch
Steps Achieved:
Distance Walked:
Calories Burned:
Mindfulness Minutes:

TUESDAY, NOVEMBER 21

Gratitude: *Appreciate Everything and Everybody*

HEALTH Watch
Steps Achieved:
Distance Walked:
Calories Burned:
Mindfulness Minutes:

WEDNESDAY, NOVEMBER 22

Affirmation: *Reinforce Self Truth*

HEALTH Watch
Steps Achieved:
Distance Walked:
Calories Burned:
Mindfulness Minutes:

THURSDAY, NOVEMBER 23

Visualization: *Create Your Actuality*

HEALTH Watch
Steps Achieved:
Distance Walked:
Calories Burned:
Mindfulness Minutes:

FRIDAY, NOVEMBER 24

Kindness: *Extend and Receive Good Deeds*

HEALTH Watch
Steps Achieved:
Distance Walked:
Calories Burned:
Mindfulness Minutes:

SATURDAY, NOVEMBER 25

Wisdom: *Share Age-Long Experiences*

HEALTH Watch
Steps Achieved:
Distance Walked:
Calories Burned:
Mindfulness Minutes:

SUNDAY, NOVEMBER 26

Spirituality: *Have a Heart Centered Mindset*

HEALTH Watch
Steps Achieved:
Distance Walked:
Calories Burned:
Mindfulness Minutes:

What I learned this week about myself, others, and/or
the world around me:

_____

_____

_____

_____

_____

_____

Exercises that I performed this week:

_____

_____

_____

_____

This week's healthy eating food choices:

_____

_____

_____

_____

NOVEMBER – DECEMBER 2023

*Joy does not come from outer circumstances but
from inward strength.*

MONDAY, NOVEMBER 27

Intention: *Focus on Desired Accomplishment*

HEALTH Watch
Steps Achieved: ....
Distance Walked: ....
Calories Burned: ....
Mindfulness Minutes: ....

TUESDAY, NOVEMBER 28

Gratitude: *Appreciate Everything and Everybody*

HEALTH Watch
Steps Achieved: ....
Distance Walked: ....
Calories Burned: ....
Mindfulness Minutes: ....

WEDNESDAY, NOVEMBER 29

Affirmation: *Reinforce Self Truth*

HEALTH Watch
Steps Achieved: ....
Distance Walked: ....
Calories Burned: ....
Mindfulness Minutes: ....

THURSDAY, NOVEMBER 30

Visualization: *Create Your Actuality*

HEALTH Watch
Steps Achieved: ....
Distance Walked: ....
Calories Burned: ....
Mindfulness Minutes: ....

FRIDAY, DECEMBER 1

Kindness: *Extend and Receive Good Deeds*

HEALTH Watch
Steps Achieved: ....
Distance Walked: ....
Calories Burned: ....
Mindfulness Minutes: ....

SATURDAY, DECEMBER 2

Wisdom: *Share Age-Long Experiences*

HEALTH Watch
Steps Achieved: ....
Distance Walked: ....
Calories Burned: ....
Mindfulness Minutes: ....

SUNDAY, DECEMBER 3

Spirituality: *Have a Heart Centered Mindset*

HEALTH Watch
Steps Achieved: ....
Distance Walked: ....
Calories Burned: ....
Mindfulness Minutes: ....

What I learned this week about myself, others, and/or
the world around me:

....

....

....

....

....

....

....

Exercises that I performed this week:

....

....

....

....

....

This week's healthy eating food choices:

....

....

....

....

....

DECEMBER 2023

Do not give your mind the opportunity to talk you out of your dream.
—Tony R. Kitchens

MONDAY, DECEMBER 4

Intention: *Focus on Desired Accomplishment*

HEALTH Watch
Steps Achieved: ....
Distance Walked: ....
Calories Burned: ....
Mindfulness Minutes: ....

TUESDAY, DECEMBER 5

Gratitude: *Appreciate Everything and Everybody*

HEALTH Watch
Steps Achieved: ....
Distance Walked: ....
Calories Burned: ....
Mindfulness Minutes: ....

WEDNESDAY, DECEMBER 6

Affirmation: *Reinforce Self Truth*

HEALTH Watch
Steps Achieved: ....
Distance Walked: ....
Calories Burned: ....
Mindfulness Minutes: ....

THURSDAY, DECEMBER 7

Visualization: *Create Your Actuality*

HEALTH Watch
Steps Achieved:
Distance Walked:
Calories Burned:
Mindfulness Minutes:

FRIDAY, DECEMBER 8

Kindness: *Extend and Receive Good Deeds*

HEALTH Watch
Steps Achieved:
Distance Walked:
Calories Burned:
Mindfulness Minutes:

SATURDAY, DECEMBER 9

Wisdom: *Share Age-Long Experiences*

HEALTH Watch
Steps Achieved:
Distance Walked:
Calories Burned:
Mindfulness Minutes:

SUNDAY, DECEMBER 10

Spirituality: *Have a Heart Centered Mindset*

HEALTH Watch
Steps Achieved:
Distance Walked:
Calories Burned:
Mindfulness Minutes:

What I learned this week about myself, others, and/or
the world around me:

_____

_____

_____

_____

_____

_____

_____

Exercises that I performed this week:

_____

_____

_____

_____

This week's healthy eating food choices:

_____

_____

_____

_____

DECEMBER 2023

Talent is what you have;
Skill is what you learn.

MONDAY, DECEMBER 11

Intention: *Focus on Desired Accomplishment*

HEALTH Watch
Steps Achieved: ....
Distance Walked: ....
Calories Burned: ....
Mindfulness Minutes: ....

TUESDAY, DECEMBER 12

Gratitude: *Appreciate Everything and Everybody*

HEALTH Watch
Steps Achieved: ....
Distance Walked: ....
Calories Burned: ....
Mindfulness Minutes: ....

WEDNESDAY, DECEMBER 13

Affirmation: *Reinforce Self Truth*

HEALTH Watch
Steps Achieved: ....
Distance Walked: ....
Calories Burned: ....
Mindfulness Minutes: ....

THURSDAY, DECEMBER 14

Visualization: *Create Your Actuality*

	HEALTH Watch
	Steps Achieved: ....
	Distance Walked: ....
	Calories Burned: ....
	Mindfulness Minutes: ....

FRIDAY, DECEMBER 15

Kindness: *Extend and Receive Good Deeds*

	HEALTH Watch
	Steps Achieved: ....
	Distance Walked: ....
	Calories Burned: ....
	Mindfulness Minutes: ....

SATURDAY, DECEMBER 16

Wisdom: *Share Age-Long Experiences*

	HEALTH Watch
	Steps Achieved: ....
	Distance Walked: ....
	Calories Burned: ....
	Mindfulness Minutes: ....

SUNDAY, DECEMBER 17

Spirituality: *Have a Heart Centered Mindset*

	HEALTH Watch
	Steps Achieved: ....
	Distance Walked: ....
	Calories Burned: ....
	Mindfulness Minutes: ....

What I learned this week about myself, others, and/or
the world around me:

_____

_____

_____

_____

_____

_____

_____

Exercises that I performed this week:

_____

_____

_____

_____

This week's healthy eating food choices:

_____

_____

_____

_____

DECEMBER 2023

Three things will last forever: faith, hope, and love. And the greatest of these is love.
—1 Corinthians 13:13

MONDAY, DECEMBER 18

Intention: *Focus on Desired Accomplishment*

HEALTH Watch
Steps Achieved:
Distance Walked:
Calories Burned:
Mindfulness Minutes:

TUESDAY, DECEMBER 19

Gratitude: *Appreciate Everything and Everybody*

HEALTH Watch
Steps Achieved:
Distance Walked:
Calories Burned:
Mindfulness Minutes:

WEDNESDAY, DECEMBER 20

Affirmation: *Reinforce Self Truth*

HEALTH Watch
Steps Achieved:
Distance Walked:
Calories Burned:
Mindfulness Minutes:

THURSDAY, DECEMBER 21

Winter: A time to store up energy
Visualization: *Create Your Actuality*

HEALTH Watch	
Steps Achieved:	....
Distance Walked:	....
Calories Burned:	....
Mindfulness Minutes:	....

FRIDAY, DECEMBER 22

Kindness: *Extend and Receive Good Deeds*

HEALTH Watch	
Steps Achieved:	....
Distance Walked:	....
Calories Burned:	....
Mindfulness Minutes:	....

SATURDAY, DECEMBER 23

Wisdom: *Share Age-Long Experiences*

HEALTH Watch	
Steps Achieved:	....
Distance Walked:	....
Calories Burned:	....
Mindfulness Minutes:	....

SUNDAY, DECEMBER 24

Spirituality: *Have a Heart Centered Mindset*

HEALTH Watch	
Steps Achieved:	....
Distance Walked:	....
Calories Burned:	....
Mindfulness Minutes:	....

What I learned this week about myself, others, and/or
the world around me:

_____

_____

_____

_____

_____

_____

Exercises that I performed this week:

_____

_____

_____

_____

This week's healthy eating food choices:

_____

_____

_____

_____

DECEMBER 2023

Christmas is a day of meaning and traditions,
a special day spent in the warm circle of family and friends.
— Margaret Thatcher

MONDAY, DECEMBER 25

Intention: *Focus on Desired Accomplishment*

HEALTH Watch
Steps Achieved:
Distance Walked:
Calories Burned:
Mindfulness Minutes:

TUESDAY, DECEMBER 26

Gratitude: *Appreciate Everything and Everybody*

HEALTH Watch
Steps Achieved:
Distance Walked:
Calories Burned:
Mindfulness Minutes:

WEDNESDAY, DECEMBER 27

Affirmation: *Reinforce Self Truth*

HEALTH Watch
Steps Achieved:
Distance Walked:
Calories Burned:
Mindfulness Minutes:

THURSDAY, DECEMBER 28

Visualization: *Create Your Actuality*

HEALTH Watch
Steps Achieved:
Distance Walked:
Calories Burned:
Mindfulness Minutes:

FRIDAY, DECEMBER 29

Kindness: *Extend and Receive Good Deeds*

HEALTH Watch
Steps Achieved:
Distance Walked:
Calories Burned:
Mindfulness Minutes:

SATURDAY, DECEMBER 30

Wisdom: *Share Age-Long Experiences*

HEALTH Watch
Steps Achieved:
Distance Walked:
Calories Burned:
Mindfulness Minutes:

SUNDAY, DECEMBER 31

Spirituality: *Have a Heart Centered Mindset*

HEALTH Watch
Steps Achieved:
Distance Walked:
Calories Burned:
Mindfulness Minutes:

What I learned this week about myself, others, and/or
the world around me:

_____

_____

_____

_____

_____

_____

_____

Exercises that I performed this week:

_____

_____

_____

_____

This week's healthy eating food choices:

_____

_____

_____

_____

WANT TO KNOW MORE?

There is an abundance of books, audio tapes, articles, and videos to keep you engaged in mindfulness. It's up to you to choose your path to a happier and more fulfilling life. The following are some of my favorites:

Videos: YouTube Resource

Go to "Select" on your YouTube Channel and type in your selection. This will save a lot of searching time. I have created a catalog of my favorites, and what I watch varies. Add your favorite. A sampling of my favorites:

- ☐ "A Grateful Mind Attracts Miracles" by Rising Higher Meditation
- ☐ "Powerful Affirmations and Powerful Gratitudes" by Bob Baker
- ☐ "Powerful Brainwave Mindfulness" by Dr. Nipun Aggarwal

Any mindfulness and gratitude video by Jess, Susie Pinon, Wayne Dyer, Louise Hay, Connie Riet, Jessica Heslop, Bob Baker, and Jason Stephenson will guide you along the way.

Some of my favorite books include:

- ☐ "Kataholos: Guidelines for a Wholistic Happy Life" by Michael Quigley
- ☐ "The Heart of China: How Mindfulness Change My Life" by Todd Cornell
- ☐ "I Know: A Practical Guide for Awakening to What's Within and Finding Work-Life Integration" by Michael S. Seaver
- ☐ Plus, any book by Joel Osteen, Rick Warren, Louise Hay, Baptist De Pape, Esther & Jerry Hicks … to name a few.

List your favorites:

- ☐ _____
- ☐ _____
- ☐ _____
- ☐ _____

Enjoy the wonderful difference this practice makes in your personal and professional life!

GLORIA PETERSEN

Gloria Petersen is a *persevering entrepreneur, unstoppable survivor, dedicated mother and grandmother*, and a *giving volunteer*. She emphasizes the importance of getting beyond personal and/or professional challenges by staying in control! Journaling is an important healing step along the way, and the first step in developing a strong sense-of-self.

Gloria is the founder and director of Global Protocol Academy, LLC. She has provided training, seminars, and coaching in professional presence, business etiquette, and international protocol for over 30 years. Her clients range from Fortune 500 companies to emerging entrepreneurs.

Gloria is now embarking on a more personal path by sharing her journey, and how she got beyond her obstacles. You can too! Watch for Gloria's next book, which is directed at helping others find their strength: "GRIT POWER ... How to Land on Your Feet No Matter What!" (*Tentative title*)

Visit Gloria's websites and join her social media for articles and tips

- Speaker and Author: GloriaPetersen.com
- Professional Development Four-book Series:
  ArtofProfessionalConnections.com
- Subject Matter Expert Training: GlobalProtocolAcademy.com

Made in the USA
Columbia, SC
06 February 2023

11205334R00096